Writers at Work

From Sentence to Paragraph

TEACHER'S MANUAL

Laurie Blass
Deborah Gordon

CAMBRIDGE UNIVERSITY PRESS
Cambridge, New York, Melbourne, Madrid, Cape Town,
Singapore, São Paulo, Delhi, Mexico City

Cambridge University Press
The Edinburgh Building, Cambridge CB2 8RU, UK

Published in the United States of America by Cambridge University Press, New York

www.cambridge.org
Information on this title: www.cambridge.org/9780521120326

© Cambridge University Press 2010

First published 2010

A catalogue record for this publication is available from the British Library

ISBN 978-0-521-12030-2 Student's Book
ISBN 978-0-521-12032-6 Teacher's Manual

ISBN 978-0-521-12032-6 Paperback

Table of Contents

Introduction

Audience

Writers at Work: From Sentence to Paragraph takes beginning-level students in either an ESL or EFL classroom through a process approach to writing. Though much of the content is personal, the writing concepts that are taught lay the groundwork for academic writing in the future.

Approach

Writers at Work: From Sentence to Paragraph achieves the elusive goal of getting beginning-level students to benefit from a writing process approach. This is done through scaffolding the writing process with a strong emphasis on vocabulary and grammar in the first steps of the process. This focus on language development serves as a foundation for writing coherent and cohesive topic-related sentences in the first seven chapters, and paragraphs in the final three chapters.

Organization of the text

Writers at Work: From Sentence to Paragraph consists of two parts:

Preview the Process

This section introduces students to the writing process and familiarizes them with the structure of a typical *Writers at Work: From Sentence to Paragraph* chapter. Students learn the importance of vocabulary, grammar, and idea connectors in clear writing. They are also introduced to a drafting process that proceeds from freewrite to first draft, to second draft, and then to final draft. They become aware of the value and techniques of peer editing and of sharing their final work with their classmates.

Chapters 1–10

Each chapter opens with a set of questions designed to get students thinking about the topic. Chapters are organized into five sections that take students through vocabulary acquisition and idea generation, review and acquisition of topic-related grammatical structures, revision and editing strategies, and sharing opportunities. These sections are described in detail.

Chapter structure

Each chapter has the following sections:

I Getting Started

Students start out by studying words and phrases related to the chapter topic that they will use in their writing assignments. You may want to read the words once or twice for students to listen and then repeat so they can learn how to pronounce them. However, it is not necessary to pre-teach these words. The activities allow for students to work together to learn them. They recognize, decode in context, and produce the new vocabulary through a variety of pair- and small-group interactive activities. These activities have two functions: They help students to learn the new vocabulary, and at the same time, they also help students to begin to generate their own ideas on the chapter topic, which they will use later in their writing.

Section I culminates in a freewriting activity. The purpose of freewriting is to encourage fluency and help students generate ideas on the topic. Freewriting is a timed activity, but other than that, it has no restrictions. Students should not worry about spelling, grammar, or organization. Freewriting is not collected or graded, or read by anyone other than the student. Remind students that their freewrites are not a draft, but rather should be seen as just an idea pool; it is recommended that you have students underline the ideas in their freewrites after they finish freewriting.

It's important that students be relaxed and comfortable when freewriting. The amount of time you give them depends on your assessment of their level. We recommend beginning with two to five minutes in Chapter 1. You can increase the time in later chapters. However, it helps to have students try to freewrite quickly, encouraging them to write as much as they can in a short period of time. To do this, you might want to have students keep a chart of the number of words they write in each freewrite. For classes with students who seem to like freewriting, you may want to assign freewriting tasks on other topics to break up the pace and to practice "fluency."

II Preparing Your Writing

In this section, students learn and practice grammar structures related to the chapter topic that they will use in their writing. Structures are presented in information boxes. Before you go over information box material, you may want to begin by writing sentences on the board that illustrate the structure, and asking students analysis questions. Have students follow along as you read through the material in the information box. Have them repeat example sentences, and elicit or provide additional examples for the points in the boxes. Specific suggestions for presenting each information box are given in the chapter notes.

Practice exercises follow each information box. You can collect and grade practice exercises, or go over answers with the class. For discrete-item exercises, you can have students compare their answers in pairs and then have volunteers share their answers with the class. For sentence-level exercises, it's often a good idea to have students write their answers on the board and discuss them as a class. For paragraph-level exercises and error correction, it is useful to put the activity on a transparency and make changes or corrections on the transparency as students call out the answers.

At the end of Section II, students combine the ideas they developed and vocabulary they learned in Section I with the grammar they've just been working on to write their first draft. In Chapters 2–7, students are given two writing assignments. We believe that providing students with two assignments gives them the optimal amount of practice for writing topic-related sentences. It also provides different contexts to practice using the new grammar and vocabulary. However, teachers may feel that for their particular class, working on just one of the two writing assignments will provide sufficient practice. In Chapters 8–10, students are given only one writing assignment. This allows them to focus on creating one cohesive, well-formed, and well-supported paragraph, which they will be doing for the first time. You can have students complete their first drafts as homework, or in class while you circulate to offer help, as needed.

Have students write as neatly as possible and on every other line, as this will be important in the feedback stage. At this stage of the book, students are not required to type their drafts, but if any students would like to, have them double-space their lines.

III Revising Your Writing

Revising is an integral part of the writing process, albeit one that can be very difficult for beginning-level students. The *Revising Your Writing* section takes students step-by-step through two level-appropriate aspects of improving and revising their writing: expanding their vocabulary and connecting their ideas. Students also give and get feedback on their revised first drafts, and then write second drafts.

Each *Expand your vocabulary* part presents an opportunity for students to acquire and consolidate new words and expressions on the chapter topic that they can use to refine and extend their ideas. New vocabulary offers students the chance to develop new ideas and consequently to add new sentences as well as make changes in their vocabulary choices.

Connect your ideas presents ways for students to combine and support ideas so that their sentences are more complex. Information boxes in this section present a variety of logical connectors such as *and*, *or*, and *for example*. This section may also result in students thinking of more ideas they would like to add to their writing.

Expand your vocabulary and *Connect your ideas* each include practice exercises and an application activity called *Your turn*. *Your turn* is an opportunity for students to write new sentences and generally make changes to their drafts using the new vocabulary or idea connectors they have been practicing. To do this, students write the changes directly on their drafts. If you do this in class, you may want to circulate to offer help, as needed.

It's important for students to get used to the idea of marking up their drafts with things that they want to add or change. Have students make notes directly on the page: in the margins, immediately above or below sentences, or at the bottom or top of the page. Have them use numbers or arrows to indicate the placement of the new information in their draft. You may also want to hand out or have students bring pens or pencils that are a different color from the one they used to write their drafts. Try to avoid red. Although it's noticeable, it sometimes means "incorrect," and these additions are anything but!

Section III also takes students through a peer feedback activity. Students read each other's first drafts and answer a series of questions about them. It's a good idea to encourage students to make an initial positive comment about their partner's work, and to make sure all comments are constructive. It can be useful to show students that it is easier to listen to advice after hearing something positive about their writing. You may want to illustrate this by modeling the process with one of the students.

To get the best results from the feedback process, have students get into pairs and exchange their books and their first drafts. Explain that they will discuss their drafts with their partner, and write the comments on the chart in their *partner's* book so he or she will have it to refer to later. Have students read their partner's paper(s) one time just to get the main ideas. After this first reading, have students underline and comment on parts that they liked about the paper. Then have students read the paper a second time and complete the chart. This time, they should be reading a little more carefully in order to answer the questions in the chart. Sometimes, students may need to explain to their partner where their new *Your turn* sentences go, and explain the reasoning behind their placement. Encourage students to ask their partners if they are not sure.

After giving and getting feedback on their first drafts, students write the second draft. Remind them to refer to the feedback charts that their partners filled in. They can write the second draft in class or as homework.

IV Editing Your Writing

This section teaches students to edit their writing for sentence-level mechanics issues, such as punctuation, spelling, and common grammatical mistakes.

Students first learn and practice a mechanics point, such as comma use. As with Section III, this section includes a *Your turn*. This *Your turn* provides an opportunity for students to look at their drafts for the specific mechanics point they have just learned and practiced. Have them check their drafts for that point only. Remind them not to get too caught up in their ideas or their sentence structure, as this will distract from the editing process. Remind students that they will have time to do this when they write their final drafts. Have students make their corrections directly on their drafts.

Students then review a common mistake related to the grammar they have learned in the chapter, such as subject-verb agreement. They edit a text correcting instances of the common error.

After this, students proceed to a cumulative, guided editing activity. Using a checklist, students check their own writing for the mechanics issues presented in this section. To do this, have students look for and check each item on the checklist. Have them make their corrections directly on their draft.

At this point, students will incorporate all their mechanics edits into a final, polished draft. Remind students that they can make additional changes if they wish, including new ideas and new sentences, as long as they carefully edit these for mechanics issues as well. As before, if students are typing their papers on a computer, tell them to double-space their lines.

V Following Up

The *Following Up* section begins with an opportunity for students to share their writing with their classmates. Sharing writing with others is a valuable activity. It emphasizes writing as communication, develops community, and provides closure. This activity could take place before the final draft is turned in, or alternatively, you could make copies of the papers before you mark them.

Each chapter ends with a *Progress Check*. It offers a chance for students to reflect on what they have learned and what they need to keep in mind going forward. Have students complete the *Progress Check* form in their books. You can have students complete them in class as you go around and offer input, or you can have students do them as a homework assignment. Alternatively, you can meet with students to personally go over their assignments and have students fill them in with you.

Preview the Process

This chapter has two functions: it introduces students to the writing process, and it introduces the basic flow of each chapter. Students get a chance to try freewriting, an aspect of the writing process that is likely to be new to them. Students also see a sample student's piece of writing in the various stages of the writing process. With your students, read the chapter introduction on page 1. Point out to students that they won't be producing any writing in this chapter, but they will be reading a sample student's writing, and they will be learning about what they will be doing in the chapters to come.

I GETTING IDEAS BEFORE YOU WRITE

A Learn new words *page 2*

Explain to students that every chapter begins with topic-related vocabulary, some of which will be familiar, and some of which will be new. Read the information box *Learning New Words* as students follow along. You might want to illustrate what a pool is by drawing a swimming pool on the board and then filling it with words. Explain that they will be choosing words from the pool to use in their writing. In each chapter, they will begin by identifying the words in the pool that they already know, and the ones they don't. They will then get into pairs to compare what they know and don't know, and they will attempt to teach each other any new words they know that their partners don't know.

Elicit from students the meaning of *parts of speech, sentence parts, writing terms,* and *mechanics*. Use the words in the pool to help you. Then explain to students that the checking and highlighting they see here is what they will be doing for themselves in the coming chapters.

Practice 1 *page 2*

Answers

| 1 9   2 9   3–5 Answers will vary.

B Freewrite *page 3*

In Chapters 1–10, there will be additional activities with the *Vocabulary Pool* items that will help students develop ideas for their own writing. Following those activities, students will freewrite. Section B of this chapter walks students

1

through the steps of freewriting and gives them an opportunity to try it out for themselves. You may find that this is the first time many of your students have encountered freewriting. To begin, explain to students that freewriting is a way for them to develop their ideas. Read the information box *Freewriting* as students follow along. Then emphasize that their freewriting will result in a "pool" of ideas similar to the "pool" of vocabulary items in the previous section. From this pool students will pick and choose ideas for their writing. Explain that freewrites are called "free" because students do not need to worry about such things as grammar, spelling, and punctuation. They don't even need to write in complete sentences. Many students at this point will be more successful just listing words and phrases. Explain that students will not have to show anyone their freewrites. For more complete instructions, see page v.

Practice 2 *page 3*

Answers

| 1 4   2–4 Answers will vary.

Your turn *page 3*

You may want to first model freewriting on the board or on an overhead projector so that students can see the process. Your freewrite could be about your own writing process and any difficulties you may have, or it could be about a completely different topic. Read the instructions while the students read along. Students are often resistant to writing phrases such as *I can't think of anything to write*. It can be useful to model this for them while you freewrite, illustrating that when you stop to think and pick up your pencil or pen, it is hard to get started again. Most students find that while writing a sentence such as *I can't think of anything to write*, new ideas occur to them, and they can go back to freewriting their ideas.

Make sure students realize that they are to continue writing until you stop them. The amount of time you give them depends on your students. It can take students up to a minute to get going, so it is advisable to give them at least two minutes. However, it could be that many students peter out by the end of two minutes. Watch your students, and if they are still writing after two minutes, let them continue until they seem to want to stop. Encourage students who want to stop writing early to keep writing even if it is only to write about not having any more ideas.

After students finish their freewrites, you may want to have them answer the questions in *Practice 2* about their own freewrites.

II STARTING TO WRITE

A Learn grammar *page 4*

Read the information box *Learning Grammar* as students follow along. Explain that each chapter will have two to four information boxes on related grammar points and that each information box will be followed by one, two, or three practice exercises.

Practice ⬛3 *page 4*

Explain that this is a practice that was already completed. Review the meaning of *subjects* and *verbs* with students, if necessary. Alternatively, have students figure it out through reading the circled and underlined words and phrases. Have students do the practice by themselves and compare their answers in pairs while you circulate to offer assistance, as needed.

B Write the first draft *pages 4–5*

This is a good time to explain the drafting process to students. Explain that the first time students write their sentences, they are writing a *first draft*. Tell students that in this book, they learn ways to improve their writing, and then they rewrite their writing using what they have just learned. Students will end up writing a second and a final draft before they are finished. This is further explained in the next section.

Read the information box *Writing the First Draft* as students follow along. This is a good time once again to emphasize that freewrites are not first drafts, but rather idea pools. Explain that students will not be writing their own draft in this chapter, but rather they will be reading a student's first draft.

For more complete instructions about what students will be doing, see page v.

Practice ⬛4 *page 5*

Go over the instructions with students before having them do the practice in pairs. You may want to project this paragraph on an overhead projector as you discuss the answers with the class.

Possible answers

| **1** 4 | **2** 4 | **3** 2 | **4** 5 |

▮ III ▮ REVISING YOUR WRITING

A Revise *pages 5–6*

Go over the material in the information box *Revising Drafts* as students follow along. Ask students what a draft is, eliciting that each time they write, it is a new draft. Many students will feel like they have already done their best the first time around and that they won't be able to improve their writing. Emphasize to students that there will be a lot of guidance in the book to show them how to revise and improve their sentences. In the chapters that follow, this section will include a section called *Expand your vocabulary*, and another called *Connect your ideas*.

Practice 5 *page 6*

It is particularly important to emphasize to students that they will first make changes on their drafts, and then rewrite them. This exercise illustrates that for students. Read the instructions with students before having them read the draft on their own, and then do the exercise in pairs. To go over the answers, you may want to project these two paragraphs on an overhead projector as you discuss with the class the changes the student made on the draft and the rewritten draft.

Answers

1 a, c, and d

B Give and get feedback *pages 6–7*

Go over the title of the section. Explain the term *feedback* and tell students that, in this book, they will be reading each other's writing and helping each other. Tell students that when they help other students, they learn more about writing, which in turn helps them in their own writing. Read the information box *Giving and Getting Feedback* as students follow along. Assure students that in this section of each chapter, they will always have questions to guide them, so they will not have to worry about coming up with suggestions of their own. Also, emphasize the need for saying something positive about their partner's writing before giving their partner suggestions.

Practice 6 *page 7*

Explain that in the chapters to come, students will read their partner's paper(s) one time just to get the main ideas. After this first reading, students will underline and comment on parts that they liked about the paper. Then students will read the paper a second time and complete the chart. Students will then discuss their charts with their partners.

Read the chart with students. Explain that in the chapters to come, these charts will help students to revise their writing.

Answers

How many words or phrases from the *Vocabulary Pool* did the student use?   6

How many connecting words, such as *also*, *and*, *but*, or *for example*, did the student use?   3

How many words did the student cross out?   8

What do you like about the student's draft? Underline one or two things.   Answers will vary.

1–2 Answers will vary.

Practice 7 *page 7*

Explain to students that the suggestions they receive from their partners can help them revise their writing, but they don't need to follow their partner's suggestions. Have students read the second draft, and talk about which suggestions they think the student used, and which she did not.

Answers will vary.

IV EDITING YOUR WRITING

A Focus on mechanics *page 8*

Explain to students that editing is different from revising. When students edit, they will be correcting grammar, spelling, and punctuation errors.

Read the information box *Focusing on Mechanics* as students follow along. Explain that students will first learn and practice a specific point, and then they will have a *Your turn* exercise in which they apply what they've learned to their own writing. They will then review a common mistake related to the grammar they have learned in the chapter. Following that, they will proceed to a guided editing activity in which they check their own writing for the mechanics issues presented in this section, once again using a checklist.

Practice 8 *page 8*

Possible answers

1 to → too
2 my → My; for example → For example; added a comma after "For example"; dont → don't; added a period after "I have other problems"; i → I; dont → don't; added a period after the last sentence
3 have → has; added "is"; a → an

B Write the final draft *page 9*

In this section in the chapters to come, students will incorporate all their mechanics edits into a final, polished draft. They will then be given a guided activity that requires them to share their writing, and read other students' writing. In this chapter, however, they look at the sample student's final draft and compare it to the student's previous drafts.

Read the information box *Writing the Final Draft* as students follow along.

Practice 9 *page 9*

Answers will vary.

Chapter 1 — All About Me

In this chapter, students will produce a short piece of writing about themselves, including information such as where they are from, who they live with, what they do, and what they enjoy or are good at. They prepare for a first draft by working with vocabulary that will help them express these ideas, as well as by learning and practicing the simple present of *be*. After that, students expand their vocabulary by learning nationality words, learn to connect ideas using *and*, and review the use of capital letters and periods. Along the way, students refine their writing, producing their second and final drafts, for which they find an accompanying image and share with their classmates.

With your students, read the chapter introduction on page 11 and discuss the questions. Model the questions and sample answers, for example:

A: Where are you from?
B: I'm from Mexico.

Give students time to think about their answers to the second, third, and fourth questions. If the class is small enough, go around and have each student give his or her answers. If the class is large, have volunteers share their answers with the class.

I GETTING STARTED

A Useful vocabulary *page 12*

Direct students' attention to the *Vocabulary Pool*. Point out the categories and make sure students understand what each means. Read each word in the pool as students follow along silently. Then read each word again and have students repeat. Point out any words that may be particularly difficult to pronounce or that may have stress issues, such as *NICKname*. You may want to bring in a map to illustrate any country words you think might be unfamiliar to students. Give models for each of the *Useful Phrases* so that students understand how they work in a sentence, for example: *My name is Susan, I'm from Chicago,* and so on.

B Vocabulary in context *page 13*

Put students into new pairs and point out the pictures at the top of the page. Explain that they are going to read about a student, Marisol Cruz, and match the reading with the correct picture. Explain the activity, making sure students understand that they must underline the words in the passage that helped them identify the picture. Call on volunteers to share their answer with the class and the words and expressions they underlined in the passage. Alternatively, you can put the passage on an overhead and underline, or have a volunteer underline, the relevant words and expressions.

Students should check the third picture. In the text, they should underline *married, student at Austin City College, Chinese food, Daniela Mercury*, and *tennis*.

C Get ideas *page 13*

Call students' attention to the pictures. Read the captions randomly and have students point to the picture each represents. Remind students that they don't have to write about everything, and if they don't want to write about a topic such as their age or their family, it's OK. Suggest to students that for each topic they choose, they think of at least one example. Model this if necessary, for example: *I have a favorite food. It's fish tacos.*

Have students share their choices with a partner. Encourage pairs to ask and answer questions about each other's information to extend the conversation.

D Freewrite *page 13*

Explain that students are going to use all the ideas they've been talking about, and any new words they remember, to freewrite about themselves. Make sure students are relaxed and comfortable. The amount of time you give them depends on your assessment of their level at this point. You may want to begin with two minutes in Chapter 1, see how students do, and then increase the time in later chapters.

II PREPARING YOUR WRITING

A Learn about the simple present of *be* *pages 14–15*

Write a few sample sentences on the board with *be* using students' names, for example: *I am a student. Claudia is a student. Peter and Giorgio are students.*

Ask if students can identify the verb in each sentence and have volunteers come to the board and underline them.

Call students' attention to the information box *Simple Present of* Be and have them follow along as you read the information. Pause to answer questions or clarify particular points. For example, have students repeat each of the forms of *be* in the chart, and point out the first- and third-person singular forms (*am, is*). For each point, elicit additional examples from the class.

Test students' understanding of the points in the information box by writing additional sentences on the board with missing forms of *be* and having students supply them, for example: *I _____ a teacher. My husband _____ from Canada.*

Practice 1 *page 14*

Remind students to pay attention to the subject of each sentence.

Answers

1 are	4 are	7 are	10 is	13 is
2 am	5 are	8 is	11 is	14 are
3 is	6 is	9 is	12 is	

Practice 2 *page 15*

Make sure students understand that they are to use the cues to create complete sentences. Point out that some sentences require *be from*.

Answers

1 Mari is from Japan.
2 Jack and Lucy are not teachers.
3 I am interested in Brazilian music.
4 We are good at sports.
5 They are not from China.

6 My favorite food is Chinese.
7 My name is Claudia.
8 Diego is from Colombia.
9 We are married.

B Learn more about the simple present of *be* *pages 15–16*

Say *I am single* and *I'm single*. Ask students if they can hear the difference. Then write the sentence with the contraction on the board. Ask students what *'m* stands for.

Call students' attention to the information box *Contractions with* Be and have them follow along as you read the information. Pause to answer questions or clarify particular points. For example, have students repeat the affirmative and negative contractions in the chart. Point out the variations in the negative forms and explain that there is no difference between the two.

Check their understanding of the points in the information box by writing a few sentences with no contractions on the board and having students come up and rewrite them with the contracted forms.

Practice 3 *page 16*

Write *I am Francisco* on the board and ask students to give the contracted form for *I am*. Then have students read the text about Francisco and explain that they are going to change all the *be* verbs to their contracted forms.

Answers

¹I'm ~~I am~~ Francisco. ²I'm ~~I am~~ from Colombia. ³I have a nickname. ⁴It's ~~It is~~ Franco.
⁵I live in Los Angeles now. ⁶I live with my family. ⁷My sister and I go to school.
⁸We're ~~We are~~ students at L.A. City College. ⁹I'm ~~I am~~ not married. ¹⁰I'm ~~I am~~ still single.
¹¹I'm ~~I am~~ interested in sports. ¹²I'm ~~I am~~ not good at tennis. ¹³It's ~~It is~~ too hard. ¹⁴I'm ~~I am~~
good at soccer. ¹⁵It's ~~It is~~ a lot of fun.

Practice 4 *page 16*

Make sure students understand that they are going to write two sentences – a
negative and an affirmative one – and that information for the second sentence
is in parentheses after each item.

Answers

1 He isn't from China. He's from Taiwan.
2 She isn't / She's not a teacher. She's a student.
3 I'm not from New York. I'm from San Francisco.
4 They aren't / They're not from El Salvador. They're from Costa Rica.
5 He isn't / He's not single. He's married.
6 She isn't / She's not from Poland. She's from Bulgaria.
7 We aren't / We're not good at tennis. We're good at soccer.
8 You aren't / You're not interested in music. You're interested in sports.

C Write the first draft *page 16*

Have students complete their first draft as homework, or in class if time permits.
Remind students to use their freewrites to give them ideas, but that their
freewrites are not a draft. Remind them also to keep in mind the rules they
learned about sentences with *be* as they write.

III REVISING YOUR WRITING

A Expand your vocabulary *page 17*

Write on the board a sentence about the country a student is from, for example:
Binh is from Vietnam. Then begin a sentence in which the country name is
replaced by the adjective nationality word (*Vietnamese*). Underline the ending
(*-ese*) and point out that these words are capitalized, just like the country word.

Go over the material in the information box *Nationality Words* as students follow
along. Have students repeat the example nationality words and elicit further
examples of each type, for example: Indian.

If the class is small, go around and have each student give the nationality word for the country they are from. If the class is large, call on a sampling of students from different countries.

Practice 5 *page 17*

Answers

1 Japanese	3 American	5 Egyptian
2 English	4 Mexican	6 Chinese

B Connect your ideas *page 18*

Write two sample sentences on the board with two similar ideas, for example: *I speak English. I speak Spanish.*

See if students can express the ideas from the two sentences in one sentence. Write the new sentence on the board: *I speak English and Spanish.*

Direct students' attention to the information box *Using* And. Go over the information in the box as students follow along. If necessary, break each sample sentence into its two sentence parts to illustrate the transformation:

I live with my husband. + I live with my two children. → *I live with my husband and my two children.*

Practice 6 *page 18*

Go over the example as a class. Remind students to write one complete sentence with all the information.

Answers

1 I work at the Holiday Inn and the Ramada.
2 I live with my mother and my father.
3 I'm a student at L.A. City College and Evans Adult School.
4 I live with my wife and my two children.
5 I speak Spanish and Portuguese.
6 I'm good at piano and guitar.
7 I like tennis and soccer.
8 I take an English class and a computer class.

C Give and get feedback *page 19*

Have students get into pairs and exchange their books and their first drafts. See page vii for more complete instructions.

D Write the second draft *page 19*

Have students use the feedback they just received to write a second draft. Remind them to refer to the charts that their partners filled in. See page vii for more complete instructions.

A Focus on mechanics *page 20*

Depending on the level of your class, you may want to begin by writing several lowercase and capital letters on the board and asking students to identify them as lowercase or uppercase.

Draw students' attention to the information box *Using Capital Letters and Periods*. Read through the information as students follow along. Elicit from the class additional examples for each of the points, e.g., additional places, names, nationalities, and languages.

Practice 7 *page 20*

Write a sample sentence on the board with the period and capital letters missing, for example: *i am from san diego, california*

Have volunteers call out the corrections and you make them on the board. Go over the first sentence together, making sure students find the other two errors in this sentence: *My name is Fernando.*

Answer

My name is Fernando. I'm Mexican. I'm from Chiapas. I go to Holyoke Community College. I work at Dash, a store in the mall. I also work at the hospital. I live in Northampton now. I live with another student, Thiago. Thiago is a difficult name for Americans. His nickname is James. James is Brazilian. He's from São Paolo. He speaks Portuguese and English. I speak Spanish and English. I'm good at sports. My favorite sports are basketball and baseball.

B Check for common mistakes *page 21*

Go over the information box *Missing Be Verbs*. Point out that this is a common error that many students make. Write additional examples on the board: *My name Susan.* → *My name is Susan. I from Canada.* → *I'm from Canada.*

Practice 8 *page 21*

Go over the first sentence with the class. Then have students check the second sentence and confirm that it is correct.

Possible answers

> [1]My name *is* Roberta Sanchez. [2]I'm Costa Rican. [3]~~I~~ *I'm* from Monteverde. [4]~~I~~ *I'm* married. [5]My husband *is* Mexican. [6]~~We~~ *We're* students at Western State University. [7]~~I~~ *I'm* a nurse. [8]My husband *is* a nurse, too. [9]~~I~~ *I'm* interested in lots of things. [10]~~We~~ *We're* in a very good rock band! [11]My favorite type of music *is* rock music.

C Edit your writing *page 21*

Have students look for and check each item on the checklist. Have them make their corrections directly on their draft.

D Write the final draft *page 21*

Have students incorporate all their mechanics edits into a final, polished draft. Remind students that they can make additional changes, if they wish.

V FOLLOWING UP

A Share your writing *page 22*

Make copies of the pictures students bring in. Find a space to exhibit each picture, and give the class time to read the writing they were given and look at all the pictures. Have them find the writer and ask questions about the picture he or she brought to class.

B Check your progress *page 22*

Have students complete the *Progress Check* and turn it in or show it to you.

Chapter 2 — Home Sweet Home

In this chapter, students will produce two short pieces of writing: one about their home or a house they have lived in, and the other about a dream or ideal home. They prepare for a first draft by working with house-related vocabulary items, as well as by learning and practicing sentences beginning with *there is* and *there are* and the present tense of the verb *have*. After that, students expand their vocabulary by learning or practicing the common prepositions of place, learn to connect ideas using *too* and *also*, and review the use of the articles *a* and *an*. With your students, read the chapter introduction on page 23 and give students time to think about their answers to the questions.

I GETTING STARTED

A Useful vocabulary *page 24*

Point out to students that the words and phrases are in alphabetical order. Bring in magazine or newspaper pictures to illustrate any pieces of furniture or appliances you think will be problematic.

Possible answers

Living Room: blinds, bookcase, bookshelf, carpet, chair, closet, coffee table, couch, curtains, desk, fireplace, mirror, rug, shelf

Dining Room: blinds, carpet, chair, closet, curtains, rug, shelf, table

Kitchen: blinds, bookshelf, chair, closet, counter, curtains, dishwasher, refrigerator, rug, shelf, sink, stove, table, towel racks

Bedroom: bed, blinds, bookcase, bookshelf, carpet, chair, closet, curtains, desk, dresser, mirror, nightstand, rug, shelf, table

Bathroom: bathtub, blinds, bookshelf, chair, closet, counter, curtains, mirror, rug, shelf, shower, sink, toilet, towel racks

Have students describe a room they know well. You may want to model this by eliciting or giving a description of your classroom. Remember that the purpose of this activity is to have students discover what they already know and what they need to know about giving descriptions. It is not recommended that you correct students' errors at this time.

B Vocabulary in context *page 25*

Check students' comprehension of the term *dream home*. After students complete the exercise, call on volunteers to share their answers with the class and the things that they underlined in the descriptions. Alternatively, you can put the page on an overhead and circle, or have volunteers circle, the relevant pictures.

Answers

| 1 c   2 d   3 b   4 a

C Get ideas *page 26*

Call students' attention to the picture of an apartment, pointing out the use of circles and squares to symbolize furniture. Read the questions under the picture and either have students answer the questions in pairs, or together as a class. Encourage pairs to ask and answer questions about each other's room descriptions to extend the conversation and use more vocabulary items.

D Freewrite *page 26*

Explain that students are going to use all the ideas they've been talking about, and any new words they remember, to freewrite about their home and their dream home. For more complete freewriting instructions, see page v.

II PREPARING YOUR WRITING

A Learn about *there is / there are* *pages 27–28*

Write a few sample sentences on the board with *there is / there are* describing your classroom, for example: *There are 25 desks in the classroom. There is a bulletin board next to the door.* Ask if students can explain why the first *be* form is *are* and the second one is *is*, eliciting that the choice of *are* and *is* is determined by the following noun or nouns. You may want to have volunteers come up to the board to circle the nouns that follow *are* and *is* and say which one is singular and which one is plural.

Call students' attention to the information box *Using* There Is / There Are and have them follow along as you read the information. Make sure they understand the way to make *there is / are* negative. Note that the form *There isn't a fireplace* and *There aren't any chairs* is not being taught at this time because of the need for the article *a* in the singular form, and the use of *any* with the plural form.

Test students' understanding of the points in the information box by writing additional sentences on the board with missing forms of *be* and have students supply them.

Practice 1 *page 27*

Remind students to pay attention to the noun following *be* and to use it to help them make their choices.

Answers

1 is	**4** is	**7** are	**10** are	**13** are
2 are	**5** is	**8** are	**11** are	
3 is	**6** are	**9** is	**12** is	

Practice **2** *page 28*

Check students' comprehension of the term *dormitory*. Have students read the writing and the questions that follow. When they finish, have volunteers write their sentences on the board and discuss their answers with the class.

Answers

1 There are two closets.
2 No, there aren't. / No, there are no couches.
3 Yes, there is. / Yes, there's / there is one window in each room.
4 There's / There is a kitchen on the first floor.
5 There's / There is a stove and two large sinks.
6 (Because) There are no tables or chairs in the kitchen.

B Learn about *has / have* *pages 28–31*

Write on the board: *There is a carpet on the floor. My classroom has a carpet on the floor.* Ask students to discuss the differences in the two sentences. Circle the verbs *is* and *has* and elicit or explain that they are both used with singular nouns. Then draw arrows to illustrate that *there is* is determined by the noun that follows, whereas *has* is determined by the noun that precedes it.

Call students' attention to the information box *Using* Has / Have. Check their understanding by writing a few sentences on the board with the *have* verb missing and having students come up and write the correct form of the verb.

Practice **3** *page 29*

Have students say which form of *have* should follow *My kitchen*. Tell students to decide first whether or not they need to find an item with *has* or *have*.

Answers

1 d	**3** i	**5** h	**7** b	**9** e
2 g	**4** a	**6** j	**8** f	**10** c

Practice **4** *page 29*

You may want to do the first item together as a class.

Answers

1 My building / has
2 All of the apartments / have
3 My bedroom / has
4 The living room / has
5 The living room / has
6 All of the rooms / have
7 The kitchen / has

Practice 5 *page 30*

Write a few sentences about your classroom on the board using only *there is / are*, then a few with only *has / have*, and then some examples with both forms.

Ask students which sounds better. Point out that you can combine the two forms and that good writing has more than one type of sentence.

Call students' attention to the information box *Using* Has / Have *and* There Is / There Are. Go over the example with the students. Then have students complete the exercise.

Answers

1 The living room has three windows.
2 The living room has a coffee table.
3 Both bathrooms have a bathtub and a shower.
4 The living room and the kitchen have blue walls.
5 The closet door has a mirror.
6 The bedroom has two nightstands.
7 My neighborhood has three apartment buildings.
8 The yard has a table and chairs.

Practice 6 *page 31*

Tell students they are going to read sentences with six *be* and *have* mistakes in addition to the example. Explain that not every sentence has an error.

Answers

---

[1]My family lives in a big house in the country. [2]There ~~is~~ *are* lots of rooms in this house. [3]The house ~~have~~ *has* five bedrooms. [4]I ~~has~~ *have* five brothers and three sisters. [5]I share a bedroom with two brothers. [6]My bedroom has three beds. [7]There ~~are~~ *is* a dresser and a big closet, too. [8]There are two desks in my bedroom. [9]My three sisters ~~has~~ *have* one bedroom, too. [10]The house ~~have~~ *has* a big yard. [11]There is a chair in the yard. [12]There ~~is~~ *are* also a lot of apples trees in the yard.

Practice 7 *page 31*

Have students read the sentences as they are. Then ask students how they sound, eliciting that they don't sound good because all the sentences use *there is / are*. Check that students understand that they are only changing six sentences and that this will improve the writing.

Answers

1 New York City has some very old apartment buildings.
3 Each floor has one apartment.
5 Each apartment has a kitchen and small bathroom.
7 The kitchen has no oven.
9 These apartments have one or two bedrooms.
11 These apartments have no dining room, either.

C Write the first draft *page 31*

For complete instructions, see page vi.

III REVISING YOUR WRITING

A Expand your vocabulary *page 32*

Write on the board the list of prepositions from the information box *Prepositions of Place*. Have students stand up and walk around the room, making sentences about things that illustrate these prepositions in your classroom. Alternatively, have students place themselves or their possessions in positions in the classroom that illustrate the prepositions, and have them ask other students to make appropriate sentences about them. After practicing the prepositions with the students, have students read the information box.

Practice 8 *page 32*

After finishing the exercise, have students compare their pictures in pairs. Alternatively, while the students draw their pictures, you can draw the pictures incorrectly on the board and have students tell you what is wrong with your pictures.

Answers

1 Students should draw a sink with a window above it. Next to the sink, students should draw a stove with a pot on it.
2 Students should draw a room with a couch, a coffee table in the middle of the room with a vase of flowers on it, and a TV in the corner.
3 Students should draw a bathtub, a window to the right of the bathtub with a shelf underneath it, and a door opposite the window. There are more shelves behind the door.

Practice 9 *page 33*

Check that students understand that there are two tasks for them to do: first, complete the sentences, and then find the object that is depicted in the sentences in the picture and number them.

Answers

1 The dresser	3 The closet	5 The telephone
2 The mirror	4 The nightstand	

Practice 10 page 33

Check students' comprehension of all the items. Then have students complete the exercise individually in class or for homework before having them compare their answers with a partner.

Answers

1 on	3 next to	5 to the right
2 in the middle of	4 under	

B Connect your ideas page 34

Write two sample sentences on the board with two similar ideas, for example: *My house has a porch. There's a yard.*

Ask students if they know of any words that can be added to the end of the second sentence to connect the ideas in the two sentences, eliciting the words *too* and *also*. Add *too* to the second sentence to make it *There's a yard, too*. Rewrite the two sentences without *too* and tell students you can do the same thing with *also*. Elicit or explain that *also* goes after *be* and before the main verb. Add *also* to the second sentence to make *There's also a yard*. Then add *It has many trees*. Have students tell you where to add *also* to this sentence, showing that *also* goes before *has*. Direct students' attention to the information box *Using* Too *and* Also.

Practice 11 page 34

Remind students to put a comma before *too*. After completing the exercise, have volunteers write their answers on the board and go over them as a class.

Answers

1 It's very comfortable, too.
2 There's also a dresser with a mirror.
3 There's a shelf, too.
4 The desk also has a big TV on it.
5 The dresser has books on it, too.
6 There are also blinds on the windows.
7 There's a chair at the desk, too.
8 There's also a picture behind the bed.

C Give and get feedback page 35

Have students get into pairs and exchange their books and their first drafts. See page vii for more complete instructions.

D Write the second draft *page 35*

Have students use the feedback they just received to write a second draft. Remind them to refer to the charts that their partners filled in. See page vii for more complete instructions.

IV EDITING YOUR WRITING

A Focus on mechanics *page 36*

Draw students' attention to the information box *Using the Articles* A *and* An. Have students look back at the chapter to find examples of *a* and *an* and to notice the first letter of the next word.

Practice 12 *page 36*

Write a sample incorrect sentence on the board, such as *I live in a apartment.*

Have volunteers call out the error. After students complete the exercise, write the incorrect sentences on the board for students to come up and correct, or project the sentences on an overhead projector and make the corrections with the class.

Answers

> [1]Raul lives in ~~a~~ *an* apartment building in ~~an~~ *a* noisy neighborhood. [2]It isn't in ~~an~~ *a* very good location. [3]It's ~~a~~ *an* hour away from school. [4]It's also ~~a~~ *an* old building. [5]The apartment is small, but it has ~~a~~ *Ø* large windows in the living room. [6]Raul also has ~~an~~ *a* nice kitchen. [7]The kitchen has ~~a~~ *Ø* long counters and ~~a~~ *an* electric stove.

B Check for common mistakes *page 37*

Go over the material in the information box *Confusing* There Is *and* There Are. Particularly confusing for students is when *there is* is followed by a singular noun joined to another noun by *and*. Write an additional example on the board, if necessary, such as *There is a dresser and two desks in the room.*

Practice 13 *page 37*

Have students compare their corrections with a partner. You may want to write the incorrect sentences on the board for students to come up and correct, or project the sentences on an overhead projector and make the corrections with the class.

Answers

> ¹My dream home is a small house in the country. ²There ~~are~~ *is* a living room
> and a dining room. ³~~There's~~ *There are* also two bedrooms. ⁴In the living room, there
> ~~are~~ *is* a couch and two chairs. ⁵Opposite the couch, there ~~are~~ *is* a fireplace and a
> bookshelf. ⁶~~There's~~ *There are* two beds and a dresser in one bedroom. ⁷There is a desk
> and a big chair in the other bedroom. ⁸There ~~are~~ *is* also a sunny kitchen and a
> big bathroom.

C Edit your writing *page 37*

Have students look for and check each item on the checklist. Have them make
their corrections directly on their draft.

D Write the final draft *page 38*

Have students incorporate all their mechanics edits into a final, polished draft.
Remind students that they can make additional changes, if they wish.

V FOLLOWING UP

A Share your writing *page 38*

You might want to have students rate the drawings on a scale of 1 to 5, with 1
being very different from the room they wrote about and 5 being very similar.
You might also want to post the writings with their corresponding pictures on
the wall for students to peruse at their convenience.

B Check your progress *page 38*

Have students complete the *Progress Check* and turn it in or show it to you.

Chapter 3 — Work, Play, Sleep

In this chapter, students will produce two short pieces of writing: one about their daily activities, and one about the daily activities of a famous person. They prepare for a first draft by working with activity-related vocabulary items, as well as by learning and practicing the present tense. After that, students expand their vocabulary by learning and practicing time expressions, learn to connect ideas using *or*, and learn to use commas with sentence-initial starting time expressions. With your students, read the chapter introduction on page 39 and give students time to think about their answers to the questions.

I GETTING STARTED

A Useful vocabulary *page 40*

Point out to students that these are common verb phrases. Also point out any words or phrases that may have stress or intonation issues, such as *GO to a REStaurant*. You may want to bring in magazine or newspaper pictures to illustrate any activities you think will be problematic.

Possible answers

> **Everyday Chores or Activities:** go home, go out, go shopping, go to bed, do chores, do dishes, do laundry, do housework, have / make breakfast, have / make dinner, have / make lunch, fall asleep, get dressed, get up, check e-mail, clean the house, pay bills, sleep in (late), stay up (late)

> **Free Time or Social Activities:** go out, go shopping, go swimming, go to a café, go to a restaurant, go to the club, go to the mall, go to the movies, get together with friends, check e-mail, listen to music, watch TV

> **Exercise Activities:** go hiking, go running, go swimming, go to the gym, play basketball, play games, play soccer, play tennis, work out (at the gym)

> **Work or School Activities:** go to school, go to work, do homework, take classes, take the bus

Have students compare their circled activities with a partner. Listen in and offer help, if necessary. It is not recommended that you spend time correcting students' errors at this time.

B Vocabulary in context *page 41*

Put students into new pairs and point out the pictures at the top of the page. Allow enough time for them to compare with their partner the activities in the passages with their own activities. Then call on volunteers to share their answers with the class.

Answers

| 1 b   2 d   3 c   4 a

C Get ideas *page 42*

Have students complete the chart for themselves in step 1. Then have them get into pairs and discuss their charts. For step 3, elicit from the class examples of famous people about whom it might be fairly easy to guess their daily activities, for example, sports figures or historical figures. Have students think individually of their own examples, but they can work in pairs to complete their charts, if they'd like. Circulate and offer help, if necessary.

D Freewrite *page 42*

Explain that students are going to use all the ideas they've been talking about, and any new words they remember, to freewrite about their daily activities and the daily activities of a famous person. For more complete freewriting instructions, see page v.

II PREPARING YOUR WRITING

A Learn about the simple present *pages 43–45*

Write a few sample sentences on the board using students' names, for example: *I go to school on Wednesdays. Claudia goes to school every day. Peter and Giorgio go to school on Mondays and Wednesdays.* Underline the verbs and ask if students can explain why the form is different in the second sentence.

Call students' attention to the information box *The Simple Present* and have them follow along as you read the information. Have students repeat the example sentences. Pause to answer questions or clarify particular points. For example, point out the forms for third-person singular regular verbs and the forms for common irregular verbs. For each point, elicit additional examples from the class.

Test students' understanding of the points in the information box by writing additional sentences on the board with missing verbs and having students supply them, for example: *I _____ at Evans Adult School. Raul _____ at 7 a.m. on weekdays. Peter _____ his homework at the library.*

Practice 1 *page 43*

Remind students to pay attention to the subject of each sentence as they do each item.

Answers

1	runs	3	work	5	check	7	do	9	play
2	take	4	starts	6	go	8	eats	10	watches

Practice 2 *page 44*

Direct students' attention to the schedule at the top of the page. Answer any questions students may have about it. Make sure students understand that they are to use the information in the schedule to complete the sentences. Explain that more than one verb may be possible for some of the sentences. When they finish, have volunteers write their sentences on the board and discuss their answers with the class.

Answers

1	gets up	4	goes	7	has / goes to / takes
2	eats / has / makes	5	eats / has / makes	8	go
3	swims	6	works out		

Practice 3 *page 45*

Call students' attention to the information box *The Simple Present – Negative* on page 44 and have them follow along as you read the information. Have students repeat the example sentences. Pause to answer questions or clarify particular points. For example, point out the negative form for the third-person singular. For each point, elicit additional examples from the class.

Test students' understanding of the points in the information box by writing additional sentences on the board with missing verbs and having students supply them, for example: *I ＿＿＿ at L.A. City College. Raul ＿＿＿ at 10 a.m. on weekdays. Peter ＿＿＿ his homework in the cafeteria.*

Do the first two items together as a class. Remind students to pay attention to the words in parentheses after each sentence.

Answers

1	sleep	9	work out
2	do not get up / don't get up	10	go
3	eat	11	does not go / doesn't go
4	do not eat / don't eat	12	works
5	meet	13	stay up
6	lives	14	goes
7	take	15	sleep
8	do	16	gets up

Practice 4 *page 45*

Have students work in pairs and discuss the differences between Antonio and Oliver. When they finish, have volunteers write their sentences on the board.

Possible answers

1 Antonio goes to the movies or to a restaurant on Saturday evenings. Oliver doesn't go to the movies or to a restaurant.
2 Oliver works on Saturday evenings. Antonio doesn't work on Saturday evenings.
3 Antonio stays up late. Oliver doesn't stay up late. Oliver goes to bed early.
4 Antonio sleeps in on Sundays. Oliver doesn't sleep in. / Oliver gets up early.
5 Oliver gets up early on Sundays. Antonio doesn't get up early on Sundays.

B Learn more about the simple present *pages 46–47*

Ask students what day it is today. Then write some true sentences on the board with a time expression that refers to the current day and underline the time expression, for example: *I teach English on Wednesdays. Wei goes to school on Wednesdays.*

Direct students' attention to the information box *Using Time Expressions with the Simple Present* and have them follow along as you read the information. Pause to answer questions or clarify particular points. Have students repeat the example sentences, and make sure they notice the prepositions that go with each of the time expressions. Elicit additional examples for each point.

Check students' understanding of the points in the information box by writing a few sentences on the board with the prepositions missing and having students come up and supply the correct preposition.

Practice 5 *page 46*

Answers

1 Marta gets up late (on) Sundays.
2 My classes are (from) 9 a.m. (to) 12 noon.
3 Marc goes to work at the Elite Café (after) class.
4 He works there (from) 2 p.m. (to) 6 p.m.
5 Susanna does homework and reads (in) the evenings.
6 The children study (before) dinner.
7 We don't get up early (on) Saturday mornings.
8 We play soccer (on) weekends.
9 Yuta goes to bed (at) 1 a.m. (on) weeknights.
10 I take English classes (at) 8 a.m. (on) Mondays.

Practice 6 *page 47*

Direct student's attention to the schedule at the top of the page and answer any questions students might have about it.

Answers

1 at	5 After	9 from . . . to
2 after	6 in	10 At
3 On	7 At	
4 from . . . to	8 before	

C Write the first draft *page 47*

For complete instructions, see page vi.

III REVISING YOUR WRITING

A Expand your vocabulary *page 48*

Introduce the concept of "general time" by writing on the board some time frames, such as 6:00 a.m.–6:15 a.m., 12:00 p.m.–12:30 p.m., and so on. Then say, *I don't get up at an exact time. Sometimes I get up at 6:00 a.m. Sometimes I get up at 6:15 a.m. I get up around 6:00 a.m.*

As you go over the expressions in the box, elicit additional examples for *in the middle of* (e.g., *the night*) and *during* (e.g., *the afternoon*). Point out that *during* can precede a time frame or an activity, such as *class*, *lunch*, and so on.

Practice 7 *page 48*

Make sure students understand that they are to use each word or phrase only once.

Answers

1 around	4 During	7 about
2 morning	5 afternoon	8 evening
3 late morning	6 late afternoon	

B Connect your ideas *pages 49–50*

Write two sentences on the board that indicate a choice, for example: *At 3:00, I go to the gym. At 3:00, I go to the library.*

Then say, *Sometimes, I go to the gym. Sometimes, I go to the library.* Ask students if they know how to connect the two choices to make one sentence, eliciting the word *or*. Then rewrite the two sentences as *At 3:00, I go to the gym or to the library.* Ask students which words from the second sentence you left out of this new sentence. Write *either . . . or* on the board and ask if students can rewrite the new sentence using both these words. Elicit or write the new sentence on the board:

At 3:00, I go either to the gym or to the library. Point out that *either* precedes the first choice. Then go over the information box *Using* Or.

Practice 8 *page 49*

After completing the exercise, have volunteers write their answers on the board and go over them as a class.

Answers

1 Claudia goes to the gym or runs in the park on Thursdays.
2 Raffi buys lunch or brings food from home on weekdays.
3 Wei takes the bus or the train to school.
4 On Saturdays, Marta goes food shopping or to the gym.
5 In the evenings, we sometimes go dancing at a club or out for a meal at a nice restaurant.
6 The students check their e-mail or text their friends after school.
7 On Sundays, I sleep in or get up early and do chores.

Practice 9 *page 50*

Read the passage together, and make sure students understand what the children do and do not do. If necessary, write each child's name on the board and list the activities as students call them out. Encourage students to write sentences with *either . . . or*.

Answers

1 Robbie plays basketball or soccer on Saturdays. / Robbie plays either basketball or soccer on Saturdays.
2 Robbie comes home or goes to his friend John's house after the game. / Robbie either comes home or goes to his friend John's house after the game.
3 Robbie takes the bus or walks home from John's house. / Robbie either takes the bus or walks home from John's house.
4 Michael takes art classes or goes swimming on Saturdays. / Michael either takes art classes or goes swimming on Saturdays.
5 Dani works at the mall or goes to the gym on Saturday mornings. / Dani either works at the mall or goes to the gym on Saturday mornings.
6 Dani stays at the mall / goes shopping with friends or goes to the movies after work. / Dani either stays at the mall / goes shopping with friends or goes to the movies after work.

C Give and get feedback *page 51*

Have students get into pairs and exchange their books and their first drafts. See page vii for more complete instructions.

D Write the second draft *page 51*

Have students use the feedback they just received to write a second draft. Remind them to refer to the charts that their partners filled in. See page vii for more complete instructions.

IV EDITING YOUR WRITING

A Focus on mechanics *page 52*

Write a sentence on the board with one of the time expressions from the information box on page 46, for example: *I go to the park after school.* Draw a circle around *after school* and ask students what happens if you start the sentence with this time expression. Elicit or point out the comma, and remind students that *after* now begins with a capital letter. Draw students' attention to and go over the information box *Time Expressions at the Beginning of the Sentence.*

Practice 10 *page 52*

After students complete the exercise, have volunteers write their sentences on the board and go over corrections with the class.

Answers

1 On weekends, Tyler works at the City Café.
2 My brother goes to the gym after work.
3 Rafael makes a big breakfast on Sundays.
4 From 1:00 to 4:00, Susanna takes English classes.
5 Li takes the bus to the library after work.
6 On Friday night, I go out with my friends.
7 Every Friday, she eats out with her boyfriend.
8 Micah plays tennis with Jon on weekends.

B Check for common mistakes *page 53*

Go over the material in the information box *Subject-Verb Agreement.* Subject-verb agreement is tricky for most students, particularly the third-person singular forms. Give students a few verbs in their base form and write on the board additional example sentences with the verb missing. Elicit the correct forms from students and discuss them before proceeding to *Practice 11*.

Practice 11 *page 53*

After students complete the exercise and compare their corrections with a partner, you may want to write the incorrect sentences on the board for students to come up and correct, or project the sentences on an overhead projector and make the corrections with the class.

Answers

¹Imad and Hicham are brothers. ²They ~~takes~~ *take* English language classes at Oxnard Community College. ³Hicham goes to school every day. ⁴Imad ~~don't~~ *doesn't* go to school every day. ⁵He ~~take~~ *takes* classes on Mondays and Wednesdays, and he works on the other days. ⁶Hicham ~~don't~~ *doesn't* have a job yet. ⁷He goes home after classes. ⁸He either does his homework or he ~~work~~ *works* on his computer. ⁹He checks his e-mail and ~~search~~ *searches* the Internet for a job. ¹⁰Imad works in a restaurant. ¹¹In the evenings, Imad ~~bring~~ *brings* home food from the restaurant. ¹²Hicham and Imad ~~doesn't~~ *don't* cook dinner. ¹³They eat the food from Imad's restaurant.

C Edit your writing *page 53*

Have students look for and check each item on the checklist. Have them make their corrections directly on their draft.

D Write the final draft *page 54*

Have students incorporate all their mechanics edits into a final, polished draft. Remind students that they can make additional changes, if they wish.

V FOLLOWING UP

A Share your writing *page 54*

You might want to review some comparison language for this activity. Write on the board and discuss expressions such as *both X and Y; we both* + verb; *X does, but Y doesn't;* and so on.

B Check your progress *page 54*

Have students complete the *Progress Check* and turn it in or show it to you.

Families

In this chapter, students will produce two short pieces of writing: one about their immediate family, and one about their extended family. They prepare for their first drafts by working with topic-related vocabulary items and by learning to use subject and object pronouns. Students also learn to express possession. After that, students expand their vocabulary by learning relationship phrases, and learn to connect ideas using *and* and *but*. They also focus on capitalization of names and family terms and common mistakes with confusing male and female pronouns. With your students, read the chapter introduction on page 55 and give students time to think about their answers to the questions.

I GETTING STARTED

A Useful vocabulary *page 56*

Review with students the difference between nouns and adjectives. Point out any words that may have stress issues, such as *great-GRANDparents*. After doing the exercises, you may want to show photos, magazine pictures, or Web site images illustrating extended family members and different generations to clarify any vocabulary items you think will be problematic. Alternatively, you could draw a family tree on the board.

Check students' comprehension of *male*, *female*, and *neutral* in the word map in step 3.

Possible answers

Extended Female: aunt, ex-wife, mother-in-law, niece, sister-in-law

Extended Neutral: cousin, in-laws

Extended Male: brother-in-law, ex-husband, father-in-law, nephew, uncle

Immediate Female: daughter, granddaughter, grandmother, half sister, mother, sister, stepmother/sister, wife

Immediate Neutral: baby, child/children, grandchild, grandparents, great-grandchildren, great-grandparents, only child, parents, twins

Immediate Male: brother, father, grandfather, grandson, half brother, husband, son, stepfather/brother

B Vocabulary in context *page 57*

Answers

> **1** Elsa   **2** Jorge   **3** Alan   **4** Emilia
>
> *Vocabulary Pool* words missing from the *Vocabulary in Context* passages:
>   in-laws, mother-/father-/brother-in-law, generation, grandfather/mother/
>   parents, grandson/daughter, great-grandchildren, half-sister/brother,
>   mother, stepfather/mother/brother, twins

C Get ideas *page 58*

Suggest that students point to a person in their family tree and explain how they
are related. Encourage students to listen carefully to their partner and add any
new relationship words, if applicable.

D Freewrite *page 58*

Explain that students are going to use all the ideas they've been talking about,
and any new words they remember, to do two freewrites: one about their
immediate family, and one about their extended family. For more complete
freewriting instructions, see page v.

II PREPARING YOUR WRITING

A Learn about pronouns *pages 58–60*

Elicit the list of subject and object pronouns from the information box *Subject
and Object Pronouns* and write them on the board. Then write a sentence on the
board with a name, followed by a sentence with a blank for the subject pronoun
and a blank for the object pronoun, such as: *Marco is my cousin.* _____ *lives near*
_____. Have the students fill in *He* and *me*. Elicit from the students that the
blanks are in the subject and object positions. Point out that using pronouns
means you don't have to repeat yourself continually.

Call students' attention to the information box and have them follow along as
you read the information. Have volunteers come up to the board to draw arrows
on the sentence there.

Test students' understanding of the points in the information box by writing
additional sentences on the board with missing subject and object pronouns,
and having students come up and supply them and draw arrows.

Practice **1** *page 59*

Remind students to pay attention to the names in each sentence and to notice
the subjects and objects in each sentence. If they get confused, have students
draw arrows from the pronouns to the people they represent.

Answers

1 Alicia and Fred	4 Fred
2 Alicia	5 the children / Max and Sarah
3 Max and Sarah	6 Max and Sarah

Practice 2 *page 59*

Answers

1 They	4 He	7 She	10 She	13 she
2 them	5 him	8 It	11 She	
3 She	6 She	9 She	12 it	

Practice 3 *page 60*

Possible answer

American actress Rachel Liu is married to actor Barry Smith. They live in Los Angeles. They have four children. Brittany is 12 years old. She is the oldest. Brad and Bart are 10 years old. They are twins. Beth is 8 years old. She is the baby of the family. During the week, Barry takes the children to school. He drives them to three different schools each day. Rachel picks them up and takes them to classes in the afternoons. On the weekends, Rachel and Barry take them to the baseball park. They all love baseball!

B Learn about possessive nouns *pages 60–62*

Illustrate the meaning of *possession* by taking something off of a student's desk and writing a sentence about it on the board, such as *This is José's pencil.* Write additional sentences on the board with possessive nouns but without the apostrophes, for example: *My brother's wife is from Santa Maria. Soraida is the girls' cousin.* See if students can find the possessive nouns in the sentences and say where the apostrophes should go. Alternatively, put the sentences on the board with apostrophes and elicit the difference between the two possessive nouns.

Direct students' attention to the information box *Possessive Nouns* and have them follow along as you read the information. Pause to answer questions or clarify particular points.

Practice 4 *page 60*

Remind students to pay particular attention to whether the possessive nouns are singular or plural. You may want to have them underline them.

Answers

¹Claire's immediate family is very big. ²That's because her parents are divorced. ³Claire has two brothers, one sister, and three stepbrothers. ⁴Claire lives at her mother's house during the week. ⁵She lives at her father's house on the weekends. ⁶Her stepmother is very nice. ⁷Her name is Phyllis. ⁸Phyllis's parents live nearby, so Claire knows them, too. ⁹All the children like to visit her parents. ¹⁰Claire's family also includes a lot of pets. ¹¹For example, Phyllis's parents have two cats, a bird, and a dog. ¹²The children's favorite pet is Tweety, the bird.

Practice 5 *page 61*

Direct students' attention to the information box *Possessive Pronouns* and have them follow along as you read the information. Put the object pronouns on the board as well so that students can have all three sets of pronouns to compare at one time.

You may want to have students do this exercise in class with the list of pronouns on the board. Have students compare answers after they finish. Have students identify the subject pronoun to which their possessive pronoun corresponds.

Answers

1 your	5 My	9 his, Their
2 my	6 his	10 your, your
3 their	7 our, Her	
4 our	8 her, her, Their	

Practice 6 *page 62*

You may want to do the first item together as a class.

Answers

1 his	5 her	9 my
2 their	6 her	10 our
3 their	7 her	11 my
4 her / their	8 My	12 my / our

Practice 7 *page 62*

Refer students back to page 57. You may want to put the students in pairs to make sentences before doing the exercise individually.

Answers will vary.

C Write the first draft *page 62*

For complete instructions, see page vi.

III REVISING YOUR WRITING

A Expand your vocabulary *page 63*

Write the relationship phrases from the information box *Relationship Phrases* on the board and see which ones students already know. Have them make true sentences about themselves with these phrases. Go over the material in the information box. Direct students' attention to the ways to make these phrases negative. Elicit additional affirmative and negative examples for each phrase.

Practice 8 *page 63*

Go over the first item as a class before having students complete the exercise individually. Sentences with *but* may be particularly tricky for some students.

Answers

1 keep in touch
2 close
3 get along, not get along
4 have a good relationship / get along well / get along
5 close
6 get along well / get along
7 keep in touch
8 not have a good relationship / not get along

B Connect your ideas *page 64*

Write two sets of sentences on the board, one that can be combined with *and* and another that can be combined with *but*. Then show how the sentences can be combined by adding a comma and the appropriate connecting word. Have students make more *and* and *but* sentences of their own. Go over the information box *Using* And *and* But, having students repeat the examples and eliciting further example sentences. Make sure students notice the placement of the comma between the two clauses. Write some sample sentences on the board without the comma and have students tell you where it goes.

Practice 9 *page 64*

Go over the first item together as a class before having students complete the exercise individually.

Answers

| 1 and | 2 but | 3 but | 4 and | 5 but |

Practice **10** *page 64*

Make sure students circle the correct connecting word and add a comma before each connecting word.

Answers

| 1 but   2 and   3 but   4 and   5 and   6 but

C Give and get feedback *page 65*

Have students get into pairs and exchange their books and their first drafts. See page vii for more complete instructions.

D Write the second draft *page 65*

Have students use the feedback they just received to write a second draft. Remind them to refer to the charts that their partners filled in. See page vii for more complete instructions.

IV EDITING YOUR WRITING

A Focus on mechanics *page 66*

Write a sentence on the board with a person's name and with a family term used as a name, such as *My brother Julio and Uncle Tomas don't get along*. Ask students to point out the use of capital letters for the name *Julio* and also for *Uncle Tomas*. Explain that the *u* in *uncle* would not normally be capitalized if it weren't being used as a name. Go over the information box *Using Capital Letters with Names and Family Terms*.

Practice **11** *page 66*

Go over the example with students.

Answers

> ¹I live with my daughter ᴹMary and her husband ᶠFred. ²Danielle is ᴹMary and ᶠFred's daughter (and my granddaughter). ³She lives here with us. ⁴We also live with my aunt. ⁵ᴬAunt ᴸLinda is 80 years old, and we take care of her. ⁶ᶠFred's cousin lives with us, too. ⁷ᶜCousin ᴶJack is divorced, and he doesn't like living alone. ⁸We're a big, happy family!

B Check for common mistakes *pages 66–67*

Go over the material in the information box *Mistakes with Male and Female Pronouns*. Test students' comprehension by writing additional sentences on the board with the adverbs missing and have students correct them.

Practice 12 *page 67*

Answers

---

¹Divorce is difficult for many families, but not for some people. ²For example, Steve is divorced. ³~~She~~ *He* and ~~her~~ *his* ex-wife, Brittany, have one child, Sophie. ⁴Steve's ex-wife is remarried. ⁵~~He~~ *She* and ~~his~~ *her* new husband also have one child, Nick. ⁶Brittany and ~~his~~ *her* husband live near Steve. ⁷Brittany and ~~his~~ *her* husband get along very well with ~~her~~ *him*. ⁸Sophie is a little older than Nick, but ~~he~~ *she* and Nick get along very well, too.

C Edit your writing *page 67*

Have students look for and check each item on the checklist. Have them make their corrections directly on their draft.

D Write the final draft *page 67*

Have students incorporate all their mechanics edits into a final, polished draft. Remind students that they can make additional changes, if they wish.

V FOLLOWING UP

A Share your writing *page 68*

You might want to review some comparison language for this activity. Write on the board and discuss expressions such as *older* and *younger*.

B Check your progress *page 68*

Have students complete the *Progress Check* and turn it in or show it to you.

<table>
<tr>
<td>Chapter
5</td>
<td># That's Entertainment!</td>
</tr>
</table>

In this chapter, students will produce two short pieces of writing: one about types of movies or books that they like and don't like, and one about popular types of TV shows in their country or culture. They prepare for their first drafts by working with topic-related vocabulary items and by learning adverbs of frequency. After that, students expand their vocabulary by learning to transform nouns to adjectives, and learn to connect ideas using *such as*. Students also learn to use underlining and italics for book, movie, and TV show titles. With your students, read the chapter introduction on page 69 and give students time to think about their answers to the questions.

I GETTING STARTED

A Useful vocabulary *page 70*

Point out to students the three categories of words and phrases for types of TV shows, movies, and books. Point out any words that may have stress issues, such as *GAME show*. You may want to bring movie ads, TV schedules, or entertainment magazines or Web site images to illustrate any genres you think will be problematic.

Have students complete step 3 with a partner.

Possible answers

1 *The Mouse Math Detective*: cartoon, detective show, educational program
2 *Can You Become a Millionaire?*: game show, reality show
3 *The Monster from Mars*: action, horror, thriller
4 *My Husband, the Cowboy*: comedy, romance, western
5 *How to Be a Better Parent*: how-to, nonfiction, self-help
6 *The Princess and the Robot*: fantasy, fiction, sci-fi

Time permitting, have volunteers share their choices in step 4 with the class.

B Vocabulary in context *page 71*

Put students into new pairs and point out the pictures on the right side of the page. First, have them discuss the pictures with their partner. Then have them read the passages carefully to themselves and work with their partner to match the pictures and the genres and to indicate the writers' likes and dislikes. Call on volunteers to share their answers with the class.

Answers

a news program
b game show
c action / science fiction movie
d historical fiction book

1 Like: b; Don't like: a, c
2 Likes: c, d; Doesn't like: a, b
3 Like: a, c; Don't like: b
4 Likes: a, d; Doesn't like: b, c

C Get ideas *page 72*

After students complete steps 1 and 2, have them get up and interview their classmates. If necessary, model the interview question: *What's your favorite kind of movie?* Circulate and offer help, if necessary. Allow time for students to discuss their favorites with at least one other classmate.

D Freewrite *page 72*

Explain that students are going to use all the ideas they've been talking about, and any new words they remember, to do two freewrites: one about types of movies or books that they like and don't like, and one about popular types of TV shows in their country or culture. For more complete freewriting instructions, see page v.

II PREPARING YOUR WRITING

A Learn about adverbs of frequency *page 73*

Write the frequency scale on the board without the adverbs. Then write a sentence on the board, such as *I _____ go to the movies.* Insert different adverbs of frequency into the blank and see if students can come up to the board and indicate where on the frequency scale they belong by making a mark on the line.

Call students' attention to the information box *One-Word Adverbs of Frequency* and have them follow along as you read the information. Have students repeat the example sentences. Pause to answer questions or clarify particular points. For example, point out the location of adverbs of frequency in sentences with *be* as opposed to sentences with other verbs. For each point, elicit additional examples from the class.

Test students' understanding of the points in the information box by writing additional sentences on the board with missing adverbs, and have students come up and supply them and indicate where in the sentences they go. For example, write a sentence such as *I watch TV,* and indicate a point on the frequency scale such as "None of the time" to elicit

never
I watch TV.
ˆ

Practice 1 *page 73*

Remind students to pay attention to the verb in each sentence and to think about where the adverb goes as they do each item. When they finish, have volunteers write their sentences on the board and discuss their answers with the class.

Answers

1 Aisha rarely watches TV news shows.
2 My friends never read newspapers.
3 We often get the news from TV comedy shows.
4 Sam usually reads the news on the Internet.
5 Some people almost never watch TV.
6 Movies about real events are usually popular.

Practice 2 *page 73*

Allow time for students to share their answers with a partner. When they finish, call on volunteers to share their answers with the class.

Answers will vary.

B Learn more about adverbs of frequency *pages 74–75*

Write sentences on the board that paraphrase the phrases in the information box *Adverbs of Frequency Phrases*, for example: *I go to the movies on Fridays and Saturdays. I watch TV Monday to Sunday.* See if students can think of other ways to say the underlined words (e.g., *I go to the movies twice a week. I watch TV every day.*).

Direct students' attention to the information box and have them follow along as you read the information. Pause to answer questions or clarify particular points. Make sure they notice the two different placements of the phrases, at the beginning and at the end of a sentence. Elicit additional examples for each point.

See if students can come up with equivalents for each phrase – for example, *in January, April, July, and September* for *four times a year* – in order to test their comprehension.

Practice 3 *page 74*

Remind students to pay particular attention to all the time words in the sentences. You may want to have them underline them. When they are finished with the practice, have them compare their answers with a partner. Then have students come up to the board and write their sentences. Alternatively, you may want to project the new sentences on an overhead projector.

Possible answers

1 Jamil watches the news on TV ~~twice a week~~. *(every day)*
2 Jamil reads the newspaper ~~every day~~. *(on Sundays)*
3 Jamil ~~always~~ takes the train to work. *(usually)*
4 Jamil ~~rarely~~ works on the train. *(sometimes)*
5 Rana ~~often~~ drives Jamil to work. *(sometimes)*
6 In the evenings, Jamil and Noor ~~sometimes~~ go to the movies. *(almost never)*
7 Jamil and Noor watch educational shows and documentaries on TV ~~on Sundays~~. *(every night)*
8 Jamil and Noor ~~often~~ watch detective shows together. *(never)*

Practice 4 *page 75*

This is a very good exercise for helping students see the value of expressing the same information in different ways. If necessary, review the one-word adverbs of frequency on page 73 and discuss their equivalents before students do the exercise. You may want to project and discuss a possible version of the passage on an overhead projector.

Possible answer

Jamil **always** gets up at 6:30 a.m. Then he turns on the TV and watches the news. He doesn't read the newspaper in the morning, except on Sundays. Jamil **usually** takes the train to work. On the train, he reads a book. He also **sometimes** works on the train. Jamil does not take the train to work every day. **Sometimes** his friend, Rana, drives him to work instead. Jamil doesn't work or read in the car. Jamil **always** takes the train home. In the evenings, he and his wife, Noor, almost never go out. They stay home and watch TV. They like to watch documentaries and educational TV programs together. Jamil also likes detective shows. He watches his favorite detective show once a week. Noor doesn't watch detective shows. She goes to bed instead.

Practice 5 *page 75*

Go over the survey with the class to make sure they understand the questions and how to indicate their answers. After they write their sentences, have them discuss their answers with a partner.

Answers will vary.

C Write the first draft *page 75*

For complete instructions, see page vi.

III | REVISING YOUR WRITING

A Expand your vocabulary *pages 76–77*

Write a noun such as *romance* on the board and use it in a sentence, for example, *I like stories about romance.* Elicit the part of speech (noun). Then ask students to provide the adjective form (*romantic*) and elicit or provide the adjective form in a sentence, for example, *I'm a romantic person.*

Go over the material in the information box *Making Nouns into Adjectives* and elicit additional examples for each of the adjective endings (e.g., *comical, bored, terrific, delicious*).

Point out that in most dictionaries, noun entries include their adjective forms. If students have their dictionaries with them, give them some nouns that have adjective forms and have them look them up and tell you the adjective forms.

Practice 6 *page 76*

Encourage students to use their dictionaries if they have them.

Answers

Noun	Adjective
animation	animated
biography	biographical
drama	dramatic
education	educational

Noun	Adjective
information	informational
music	musical
mystery	mysterious
science	scientific

Practice 7 *page 76*

Answers

1 informational
2 scientific / educational
3 educational / animated
4 musical
5 dramatic

B Connect your ideas *pages 77–78*

Write two sentences on the board about entertainment preferences, such as the following: *I like reality shows. I like Survivor and American Idol.*

Ask students about the relationship between the two sentences (the first sentence states a preference; the second sentence gives examples of the preference) and if they can think of a way to join them. Ask them to try to combine them using *such as*, and elicit or provide the new sentence: *I like reality shows, such as Survivor and American Idol.*

Go over the information box *Using Such As*, having students repeat the example and eliciting additional example sentences. Make sure students notice the

40 Chapter 5

placement of the comma. Write some sample sentences on the board without the comma and have students tell you where it goes.

Practice 8 *page 77*

Do the first item together as a class. After completing the exercise, have volunteers write their answers on the board and go over them with the class.

Possible answers

1 I often watch reality shows, such as <u>I Want to be a Millionaire</u> and <u>Storm Chasers</u>.
2 Many older people like to watch news programs, such as <u>The Nightly News</u>.
3 Horror movies, such as <u>Nightmare Street</u> and <u>Monsters Under the Sea</u>, are often on TV late at night.
4 Biographies, such as <u>My Life</u>, are very popular.
5 My son likes to read children's adventure stories, such as <u>Escape from Bald Mountain</u>.
6 He usually reads history books, such as <u>The Middle Ages</u>, for school.

C Give and get feedback *page 78*

Have students get into pairs and exchange their books and their first drafts. See page vii for more complete instructions.

D Write the second draft *page 78*

Have students use the feedback they just received to write a second draft. Remind them to refer to the charts that their partners filled in. See page vii for more complete instructions.

IV EDITING YOUR WRITING

A Focus on mechanics *page 79*

Write a sentence on the board with one or two TV show, movie, or book titles in it without the underlining. Ask students to point out the titles and explain how they know they are titles (e.g., they're capitalized). Ask if students know of other ways to indicate a title in writing.

Draw students' attention to and go over the information box *Using Underlining and Italics*. If you have a computer in class, demonstrate the formatting options in Microsoft Word if students are unfamiliar with it. Alternatively, have students practice this at home or the next time they go to the computer lab, and report back on their experience.

Practice 9 *page 79*

Make sure students can distinguish between the names and the titles in this passage. Time permitting, this is a good exercise to project on an overhead projector and have students call out the titles that need to be underlined.

Answers

[1]I am in a book club. [2]We meet every six weeks to discuss books. [3]We enjoy reading historical novels by women, such as Wuthering Heights, Wide Sargasso Sea, and The Other Boleyn Girl. [4]Sometimes we read novels by men, too. [5]We read books by Cormac McCarthy, such as The Road, and books by Pat Conroy, such as The Water Is Wide. [6]We also like reading sci-fi books, such as Dune and Brave New World. [7]We often read fantasy novels, too. [8]We like The Lord of the Rings and other books by J. R. R. Tolkien. [9]We also like J. K. Rowling's books, especially the first one, Harry Potter and the Philosopher's Stone. [10]We rarely read nonfiction. [11]Sometimes we watch movies together, too. [12]We watch movies of the books we read, such as My Sister's Keeper, The Time Traveler's Wife, and Inkheart.

B Check for common mistakes *page 80*

Go over the material in the information box *Placement of Adverbs*. Test students' comprehension by writing additional sentences on the board with the adverbs missing and having them correct them.

Practice 10 *page 80*

After students complete the exercise and compare their corrections with a partner, you may want to write the incorrect sentences on the board for students to come up and correct, or project the sentences on an overhead projector and make the corrections with the class.

Possible answers

> ¹My family does different things in the evenings. ²My parents ~~go~~ *(often)* to the movies on weekends. ³They *(usually)* ~~are~~ excited about sci-fi movies, such as *Star Trek* and *The Matrix*. ⁴*(Almost never)* my grandparents ~~go~~ to the movies. ⁵They usually stay home and watch TV. ⁶My sister and I rarely stay home on weekends. ⁷We love the movies, but we don't like the same kind of movies. ⁸I like musicals, such as *Hairspray* and *Mamma Mia*. ⁹My sister ~~goes~~ to musicals *(never)* ¹⁰She *(every week)* ~~goes~~ to scary horror movies, such as *Friday the 13th*. ¹¹My little brother ~~goes~~ *(almost never)* out in the evenings. ¹²He ~~watches~~ cartoons *(always)* on TV. ¹³He also ~~watches~~ reality shows, such as *The Amazing Race,* *(often)*

C Edit your writing *page 81*

Have students look for and check each item on the checklist. Have them make their corrections directly on their draft.

D Write the final draft *page 81*

Have students incorporate all their mechanics edits into a final, polished draft. Remind students that they can make additional changes, if they wish.

V FOLLOWING UP

A Share your writing *page 81*

You might want to review some comparison language for this activity. Write on the board and discuss expressions such as *both X and Y; we both* + verb; *X does, but Y doesn't*; and so on.

B Check your progress *page 82*

Have students complete the *Progress Check* and turn it in or show it to you.

Chapter 6

People

In this chapter, students will produce two short pieces of writing: one about a person they know, and the other about a famous person. They prepare for a first draft by working with adjectives for describing people's appearance and personality traits, as well as by learning and practicing how to use adjectives and intensifiers. After that, students expand their vocabulary by learning how to use synonyms instead of repeating the same word. They also learn to provide supporting details for their main ideas with *for example*, and they learn to distinguish between spoken and written language. With your students, read the chapter introduction on page 83 and give students time to think about their answers to the questions.

I GETTING STARTED

A Useful vocabulary *page 84*

Point out to students that the words and phrases in the *Vocabulary Pool* are in alphabetical order. You may want to elicit from students that this is a list of adjectives used for describing. You may want to bring in magazine or newspaper pictures to illustrate any adjectives that you think will be particularly problematic.

Have students complete the chart individually and then compare answers with a partner, or have them complete it in pairs and discuss their choices as they go along.

Possible answers

Words that Describe Appearance: athletic, average looking, average-sized, beautiful, casual, cute, elderly, fashionable, good-looking, handsome, medium height, messy, middle-aged, neat, pretty, short, strong, tall, thin, young

Words that Describe Hair: bald, blond, curly, dark, light, long, messy, neat, straight

Words that Describe Personality: brave, calm, confident, considerate, cooperative, energetic, friendly, funny, generous, happy, helpful, independent, intelligent, kind, outgoing, patient, quiet, serious, shy, sociable, talented, thoughtful

Have students describe a person they know well. You may want to model this by eliciting or giving a description of someone familiar to the students. Remember that the purpose of this activity is to have students discover what they already know and what they need to know about describing people. It is not recommended that you spend time correcting students' errors at this time.

B Vocabulary in context *page 85*

After students complete the exercise, call on volunteers to share their answers with the class. You may want to have students describe the two people in the picture who are not described.

Answers

| 1 e | 2 b | 3 g, h | 4 d | 5 c |

C Get ideas *page 86*

Model this activity by drawing the face of a friend on the board. Explain to students that they needn't spend much time with this, but that they should draw some distinguishing features, such as curly or long hair or glasses. Have students discuss their pictured people in pairs. Encourage pairs to ask and answer questions about each other's pictures to extend the conversation and use more vocabulary items. Circulate and offer help, if necessary.

D Freewrite *page 86*

Explain that students are going to use all the ideas they've been talking about, and any new words they remember, to freewrite about a person they know and a famous person. For more complete freewriting instructions, see page v.

II PREPARING YOUR WRITING

A Learn about adjectives *pages 87–88*

Write a couple of sample sentences on the board with adjectives, for example: *My husband has curly hair. Katie Holmes is tall.* Ask students to say what kind of words *curly* and *tall* are. Elicit that these words describe nouns, and ask students which nouns *curly* and *tall* describe in these sentences. Point out the placement of the adjectives in the two different sentences, explaining that adjectives go before the nouns they describe unless they follow *be* or other linking verbs.

Call students' attention to the information box *Adjectives* and have them follow along as you read the information. Make sure they understand the linking feature of verbs like *be*, *seem*, and *look*. Also, check that students understand the meaning of *seem* and that it is used when you are not sure of something. Have students make additional sentences of their own.

Practice 1 *page 87*

Check that students know who George Clooney is. Remind students to pay attention to the verbs in the sentences with adjectives. You may want to put the sentences onto an overhead projector and go over the answers with the class.

Answers

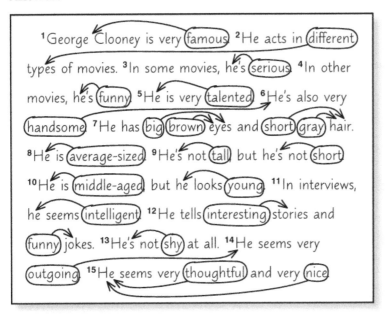

Practice 2 *page 88*

When students finish, have them compare their answers in pairs. You may want to have volunteers write their sentences on the board and discuss their answers with the class.

Possible answers

1 Her hair is short and dark.
2 Her eyes are brown.
3 His hair is blond.
4 He is average looking.
5 She is outgoing and friendly.
6 He is fairly quiet and shy, and he's extremely considerate of others.
7 They have a very happy marriage.

Practice 3 *page 88*

Emphasize that students do not know the two people pictured, so for the information they are not sure about, they should use *seem* and *look*. Have students compare their sentences in pairs. You might also have students read their sentences while the other students guess which picture they are describing.

Possible answers

> Louise is very beautiful. She has long curly hair. She wears glasses. She has a big smile. Her hair is brown. She seems friendly. She's average-sized. She looks nice.

> Rob is not handsome. He's bald. He wears glasses. He doesn't seem happy. He looks sad. He's a little bit short. He weighs 190 pounds. He's a little bit overweight.

B Learn more about adjectives *pages 89–90*

Choose three students – one of whom is a little tall, one of whom is very tall, and one of whom is extremely tall – and write on the board: _____ *is tall.* _____ *is very tall.* _____ *is extremely tall.* Ask students to discuss the differences in the three sentences. Point out the position of the intensifiers and draw arrows from the intensifiers to the adjectives they modify.

Call students' attention to the information box *Intensifiers.* Check their understanding of the points in the information box by writing a few sentences on the board about familiar people or things with the intensifier missing and having students come up and write appropriate intensifiers.

Practice 4 *page 89*

You may want to do the first item together as a class. Explain that all the sentences begin with the first word given.

Answers

1 Marco is an extremely athletic player.
2 The students wear fairly casual clothes.
3 The twins have a very outgoing mother.
4 Claudia seems fairly quiet.
5 Wei is a very nice guy.
6 Our teacher is extremely helpful.
7 My brother isn't very thin.
8 Inga is fairly sociable.
9 Yuta doesn't have very long hair.

Practice 5 *page 90*

You may choose to have students first talk about the pictures in pairs, comparing the adjective-intensifier pairs they want to use about each person. Then have students complete the exercise individually.

Possible answers

Jim's a very thin man. He's an extremely good basketball player. He's 22 years old. He's extremely tall. He's not very smart.

Eric's short and fat. He's middle-aged. He's 51 years old. He's a businessman. He's extremely smart. He's a very good cook.

Sam's very old. He's 83 years old. He's average-sized. He's fairly smart. He's extremely generous.

C Write the first draft *page 90*

For complete instructions, see page vi.

III REVISING YOUR WRITING

A Expand your vocabulary *pages 91–92*

Write the words *little* and *small* on the board and ask students if they are similar or different in meaning, eliciting that they are similar and that they are synonyms. Ask students if they know any other synonyms and write them on the board. Call students' attention to the information box *Synonyms*. Tell students that it is better to use different words rather than the same word over and over again. If you are in a room with a computer, show students how to use the thesaurus feature in Microsoft Word and how to find a thesaurus on the Internet.

Practice 6 *page 91*

After finishing the exercise, have students compare their answers in pairs. Alternatively, if possible, you may want to do this activity together as a class on a computer.

Possible answers

1 **pretty**: attractive, beautiful
2 **nice**: pleasant, kind
3 **intelligent**: clever, bright

4 **interesting**: fascinating, remarkable
5 **happy**: joyful, cheerful

Practice 7 *page 92*

Have students read the passage first before rereading it to complete the exercise.

Possible answers

B Connect your ideas *pages 92–93*

Write a general and a supporting sentence on the board, for example: *Marcia is very friendly. For example, she often invites people to her house for dinner.*

Point out that the second sentence explains the first sentence by giving specific information about it. Put on the board other general statements and have students provide supporting sentences starting with *for example*. Direct students' attention to the information box *Using* For Example.

Practice 8 *page 92*

You might want to have students make additional example sentences for each sentence in the numbered column.

Answers

| 1 f | 2 e | 3 d | 4 c | 5 a | 6 b |

Practice 9 *page 93*

Remind students to put a comma after *for example*. While students are comparing their answers in pairs, or as students finish the exercise, you might want to have volunteers write their sentences on the board.

Possible answers

1 For example, they have big dinner parties a lot.
2 For example, she doesn't talk very much at parties.
3 For example, my neighbors are elderly and the people across the street are elderly.
4 For example, they paint very well.
5 For example, they don't get angry when the students are bad.
6 For example, he never plays alone.
7 For example, he only gives his children oranges for their birthdays.
8 For example, he always gives me a ride home after school.
9 For example, she can't carry heavy things.
10 For example, he always throws his clothes on the floor.

C Give and get feedback *page 94*

Have students get into pairs and exchange their books and their first drafts. See page vii for more complete instructions.

D Write the second draft *page 94*

Have students use the feedback they just received to write a second draft. Remind them to refer to the charts that their partners filled in. See page vii for more complete instructions.

IV EDITING YOUR WRITING

A Focus on mechanics *pages 95–96*

Write a commonly misspelled word on the board, such as *windo* or *blackbord*. Ask students what is wrong with these words. Ask them if they know how to check their spelling. Draw students' attention to the information box *Checking Spelling*. If possible, demonstrate these spell-checking instructions on a computer.

Practice 10 *page 95*

Ask students if they know who Joseph Gordon-Levitt is. If not, you may want to bring in a picture from the Internet. You may want to find the first spelling error together. After students complete the exercise, write the incorrect sentences on the board for students to come up and correct, or project the sentences on an overhead projector and make the corrections with the class.

Answers

> [1]Joseph Gordon-Levitt is a talented young actor. [2]He's not very tall, but he's very good-looking. [3]He has short dark hair and ~~beatiful~~ *beautiful* eyes. [4]In some movies, he is very funny, but in some movies, he's very serious. [5]For example, in the movie *500 Days of Summer*, he's funny and serious. [6]In the magazines, his clothes are casual but ~~extremily~~ *extremely* fashionable. [7]He also seems ~~intresting~~ *interesting* and ~~inteligent~~ *intelligent*. [8]He tells jokes a lot, and seems like an outgoing, ~~frendly~~ *friendly* person.

Practice 11 *page 96*

It's very important to reemphasize to students that the suggestions the computer gives them will not always be correct. You may want to do the first one together.

Answers

1 (busy) bossy, buss, bushy		5 (curly) curler, curlew, curled, Corley
2 (healthy) health, hearty, fealty, realty		6 (comfortable) conformable
3 (famous) farmhouse, farmhouses		7 (nervous) pervious
4 (positive) positives		8 (wealthy) withy

B Check for common mistakes *pages 96–97*

Go over the material in the information box *Using Writing Words, Not Speaking Words*. Check that students are familiar with all of the intensifiers given.

Practice 12 *page 97*

Have students complete the exercise individually before comparing answers.

Possible answers

> ¹My boyfriend, Chang-hee, is a great person. ²He's ~~so~~ *very* smart. ³He speaks three languages, and he gets good grades in every class. ⁴He's ~~totally~~ *extremely* good-looking, too. ⁵He has dark hair, and he's ~~pretty~~ *fairly* tall. ⁶Chang-hee is ~~so~~ *very* nice to everybody. ⁷He's very friendly, and he's also ~~so~~ *very* helpful. ⁸All of my friends like him.

C Edit your writing *page 97*

Have students look for and check each item on the checklist. Have them make their corrections directly on their draft.

D Write the final draft *page 97*

Have students incorporate all their mechanics edits into a final, polished draft. Remind students that they can make additional changes, if they wish.

V FOLLOWING UP

A Share your writing *page 98*

You might want to model this process with yourself and two other students before students do it on their own. You also might want to give students a fixed amount of time to read each writing.

B Check your progress *page 98*

Have students complete the *Progress Check* and turn it in or show it to you.

Chapter 7 Jobs and Careers

In this chapter, students will produce two short pieces of writing: one about a job they want to have in the future, and one about a job they have or someone they know has now. They prepare for their first drafts by working with topic-related vocabulary items and by learning about count and non-count nouns. After that, students expand their vocabulary by learning phrases for talking about jobs. Students also learn to connect ideas using *because* and *so*, and to repair sentence fragments. With your students, read the chapter introduction on page 99 and give students time to think about their answers to the questions.

I GETTING STARTED

A Useful vocabulary page 100

Make sure students see the connection among the three columns *Jobs*, *Actions*, and *Work With*; that is, the columns represent sentence parts. For example: A chef (*Job*) develops (*Actions*) menus (*Work With*). You may want to bring newspaper or magazine pictures to class to illustrate any terms you think will be problematic.

Possible answers

A(n) . . .	does this . . .	with . . .
accountant	is responsible for / manages	money
administrative assistant	assists / gives	people / information
architect	designs	buildings
chef	prepares / develops	food / menus
computer technician	fixes / repairs	computers
contractor	builds	houses
cook	cooks / prepares	food / ingredients
doctor	cures / takes care of / diagnoses	patients / diseases
fashion designer	designs	clothes
gardener	is responsible for / designs	gardens
home health aide	assists / takes care of	people / patients
lab technician	performs / diagnoses	tests / diseases
landscaper	is responsible for / designs	gardens
nurse	takes care of / gives	patients / advice

A(n) . . .	does this . . .	with . . .
teacher	teaches	children / people / adults / students
veterinarian	takes care of / treats	animals
Web designer	creates / designs / develops / manages	Web sites

B Vocabulary in context *page 101*

Answers

1 d, nurse
2 b, landscaper / gardener

3 e, veterinarian
4 c, chef

C Get ideas *page 102*

Go over any quiz items that might need clarification, and then have students complete the quiz individually.

D Freewrite *page 102*

Explain that students are going to use all the ideas they've been talking about, and any new words they remember, to do two freewrites: one about jobs they want to have in the future, and one about a job they have or someone they know has now. For more complete freewriting instructions, see page v.

II PREPARING YOUR WRITING

A Learn about count and non-count nouns *pages 103–104*

Write a topic-related sentence on the board with the singular and plural forms of the same noun, such as *I had two jobs last year, but I only have one job now.*

Underline the two nouns and elicit the difference from students (one is singular and one is plural). Ask them how the form of the two nouns is different (the plural form has an *-s* ending). Then elicit the plural form of one or two irregular plurals such as *woman* (*women*) and *child* (*children*).

Finally, write sentences with a count noun and a non-count noun, such as *I don't have a job right now, so I need some work.* See if students can tell you why there is no *a* before *work* (*work* is a non-count noun; you can't count it).

Call students' attention to the information box *Count and Non-Count Nouns* and have them follow along as you read the information. Have students repeat the example words and sentences.

Practice 1 *page 103*

Have students use their dictionaries for this exercise. Time permitting, project a dictionary page with an entry for one of the count or non-count nouns in the activity, and review dictionary skills, such as using guide words and interpreting abbreviations and other entry information.

Answers

1 C, hotels	6 NC	11 NC
2 NC	7 C, nurses	12 C, cashiers
3 C, diseases	8 NC	13 C, aides
4 C, chefs	9 NC	14 NC
5 NC	10 C, technicians	

Practice 2 *page 104*

Make sure students use their dictionaries for this activity.

Answers

1 Landscapers, P	4 sunshine, NC	7 plants, P
2 an artist, S	5 things, P	8 work, NC
3 plants, P	6 art, NC	9 time, NC

B Learn more about count and non-count nouns *pages 104–105*

Write *a/an*, *the*, and (Ø) (a zero with a slash through it). Explain that Ø means "nothing." Then write sentences on the board with three types of nouns: one that is preceded by *a/an*, one that is preceded by *the*, and one that is not preceded by an article, such as the following:

I want to be _____ landscaper.
I know _____ landscaper at our school.
_____ Landscapers work outdoors.

Direct students' attention to the information box *Articles A/An, The, or Ø (No Article)* and have them follow along as you read the information.

To test their comprehension, give students sentences with nouns that must be preceded by *a* or no article, and see if they can revise them so that they are preceded by *the*. For example:

Nurses make a lot of money. → *The nurses at General Hospital make a lot of money.*

Have them underline the information in the new sentence that makes the use of *the* necessary.

Practice 3 *page 105*

When students are finished, have them compare their answers with a partner. Then elicit answers from the class. For each answer, have students explain why they chose *a/an*, *the*, or no article.

Answers

1	1 Ø	2 an	3 Ø	4 The	5 Ø	6 Ø / the
2	1 an	2 a	3 The	4 the	5 the	6 the
3	1 a	2 Ø	3 the	4 the	5 The / A	6 a
4	1 a	2 Ø	3 a	4 The	5 a / the	
5	1 Ø	2 Ø	3 an / the	4 an / the	5 Ø / the	

C Write the first draft   *page 105*

For complete instructions, see page vi.

III REVISING YOUR WRITING

A Expand your vocabulary   *pages 106–107*

See if students can think of any phrases with the word *work* in them and write them on the board. Give examples of jobs that involve working with one's hands, and see if students can guess the expression.

Go over the material in the box and elicit additional examples for each expression.

Practice 4   *page 106*

Possible answers

1 chef, computer technician, contractor, cook, home health aide, lab technician, landscaper, Web designer
2 architect, chef, contractor, cook, doctor, fashion designer, home health aide, nurse, teacher, veterinarian, Web designer
3 chef, computer technician, cook, contractor, doctor, fashion designer, gardener, landscaper
4 architect, fashion designer, teacher, Web designer
5 administrative assistant, doctor, home health aide, nurse, teacher
6 accountant, administrative assistant, architect, chef, contractor, cook, lab technician, teacher
7 contractor, gardener, landscaper
8 accountant, administrative assistant, architect, chef, computer technician, cook, doctor, fashion designer, home health aide, lab technician, nurse, teacher, veterinarian, Web designer

Practice 5   *page 107*

Answers

1 work with numbers	4 work outside	7 work with children
2 work outside	5 work with her hands	8 work on a team
3 works alone	6 work with ideas	

B Connect your ideas *pages 107–108*

Write two sentences on the board expressing a job preference and a reason for it, such as: *I want to be a landscaper. I like to work outdoors.*

Ask students what the relationship between the two sentences is (the first sentence states a preference and the second sentence gives a reason for the preference) and if they can think of a way to join them. Elicit or provide the new sentence: *I want to be a landscaper because I like to work outdoors.*

Go over the information box *Using* Because *and* So, having students repeat the examples and eliciting further example sentences. Make sure students notice the placement of the comma in sentences with *so.*

Practice 6 *page 108*

Go over the first item together as a class.

Answers

1	e, Georgio works very hard,	5	b
2	g	6	c
3	a, Suk loves sports,	7	h
4	f, Everyone loves Kaori's cooking,	8	d, Thomas loves biology,

Practice 7 *page 108*

Answers

1 makeup, so	3 because	5 exciting, so
2 because	4 because	

C Give and get feedback *page 109*

Have students get into pairs and exchange their books and their first drafts. See page vii for more complete instructions.

D Write the second draft *page 109*

Have students use the feedback they just received to write a second draft. Remind them to refer to the charts that their partners filled in. See page vii for more complete instructions.

IV EDITING YOUR WRITING

A Focus on mechanics *page 110*

Write two sentences on the board, one correct and one a sentence fragment. See if students can identify the fragment, for example: *I want to be a computer technician. Because I like to work with computers.*

Go over the information box *Fragments*. To check their understanding, write additional examples of fragments on the board and have students correct them.

Practice 8 *page 110*

Answers

1 Bao doesn't like to organize things, *s*~~So~~ he doesn't want to be a manager.
2 Mya likes to work with food, *s*~~So~~ she wants to be a chef.
3 Soraida wants to become a kindergarten teacher, *b*~~Because~~ she loves children.
4 Nali is a talented artist, *s*~~So~~ she draws pictures for books.
5 Yuta doesn't want to be a gardener, *b*~~Because~~ he doesn't like to get dirty.

Practice 9 *page 110*

Possible answers

1 Marta is very creative, so she wants to be a fashion designer.
2 Rob wants to be a contractor because he likes to build things.
3 I like to help people, so I want to be a doctor.
4 Wei wants to be a computer technician because he likes to work with computers.
5 Alex wants to be a veterinarian because he likes animals.

B Check for common mistakes *page 111*

Article errors are common for many students. Go over the material in the information box *Mistakes with Articles*. If necessary, write additional sentences on the board with article errors and discuss them with the class before proceeding to *Practice 10*.

Practice 10 *page 111*

Answers

---

¹My friend is ~~the~~*a* home health aide because she likes to help ~~the~~*Ø* people. ²She also likes to work indoors. ³~~The~~*Ø* home health aides work in ~~a~~*Ø* people's homes. ⁴They work with elderly people. ⁵~~The~~*Ø* home health aides prepare ~~a~~*Ø* healthy food for them. ⁶They give ~~a~~*Ø* medicine, and sometimes they give ~~an~~*Ø* advice. ⁷My friend cares about people, so she is ~~the~~*a* good home health aide.

C Edit your writing *page 111*

Have students look for and check each item on the checklist. Have them make their corrections directly on their drafts.

D Write the final draft *page 112*

Have students incorporate all their mechanics edits into final, polished drafts. Remind students that they can make additional changes, if they wish.

V FOLLOWING UP

A Share your writing *page 112*

Give students time to think of additional reasons for their interest in a particular job or career. You might suggest that Group B take notes on what they want to say to their Group A partner.

B Check your progress *page 112*

Have students complete the *Progress Check* and turn it in or show it to you.

Chapter 8

Important Life Events

Note that from this chapter onward, the focus changes from producing linked sentences to producing a paragraph. In Chapters 8, 9, and 10, various features of paragraphs are taught in a section titled *Learn About Paragraphs*. In this chapter, students produce a paragraph about the important events they've experienced in their lives so far. They prepare for their first drafts by working with topic-related verbs and verb phrases and by learning about forming sentences in the simple past with regular and irregular verbs and some commonly used time phrases. After that, students expand their vocabulary by learning about adverbs, and by learning to connect their ideas using *then*, *next*, and *after that* to show the order of events. Finally, students learn about the format of a paragraph and to correct common grammatical errors with the simple past. With your students, read the chapter introduction on page 113 and give students time to think about their answers to the questions.

I GETTING STARTED

A Useful vocabulary *page 114*

Point out that the words and phrases are organized alphabetically. Elicit from students that all the words and phrases are verbs or verb phrases having to do with life milestones or important events in a person's life. Point out any phrases that may have stress issues, such as the difference between *get MARried* and *MEET someone*.

Check that students understand the different categories in the chart in step 3. Explain that they should put the vocabulary items into the *General Life* category only if they don't fit into one of the others.

Possible answers

General Life: be born, die, get a pet, get sick, grow up, immigrate, move

Relationships: break up with, fall in love, get divorced, get engaged, get married, get remarried, have children, meet someone

Learning: finish school, get a degree, get a scholarship, go to college, go to school, graduate, learn to drive, start school

Work: change jobs, get a job, get promoted, lose a job, quit a job, retire

B Vocabulary in context *page 115*

Put students into new pairs. Call on volunteers to share their answers with the class.

Answers

1 Francisco's Life:	1 e	2 d	3 b	4 a	5 c
2 My Life:	1 b	2 d	3 e	4 a	5 c

C Get ideas *page 116*

Have students complete their own time lines before putting them in pairs to discuss their time lines with their partners. Circulate and offer help, if necessary.

D Freewrite *page 116*

Explain that students are going to use all the ideas they've been talking about, and any new words they remember, to freewrite about the important events in their life. For more complete freewriting instructions, see page v.

II   PREPARING YOUR WRITING

A Learn about the simple past *pages 117–119*

Write a topic-related sentence on the board in the present and the past, such as: *I live in Sanford now. I moved to Sanford in 2010.* Have students tell you what the two verbs are and what the difference between them is, eliciting the *-ed* form of *moved.* Explain that *live* is in the present but *moved* is in the past.

Call students' attention to the information box *The Simple Past* and have them follow along as you read the information. Pause to answer questions or clarify particular points. Explain to students that some verbs are regular and others are irregular and that for the moment, they will be focusing on only regular verbs. You may want to have students make sentences of their own in the past using the verbs in the box. Go over the spelling rules with students.

Practice 1 *page 117*

Have students review the verbs before they start the exercise. You may want to have them tell you which verbs follow the patterns in the spelling rules part of the information box. When they finish, have students compare their answers in pairs.

Answers

1 walked	5 moved	9 finished
2 worked	6 carried	10 traveled
3 lived	7 planned	
4 immigrated	8 played	

Practice 2 *page 118*

Have students notice the time phrases in the sentences in *Practice 1* on page 117. Ask if they know any more common time expressions, and write them on the board as they provide them. Then call students' attention to the information box *Time Expressions with the Simple Past*. Look at the different categories with students and have them produce their own true example sentences with the different time expressions. Point out the use of the comma and have students find the commas in the sentences with time phrases in *Practice 1*.

Go over the instructions for *Practice 2* and the first sentence, checking that students understand how to find the first word of the sentence. You may want to project the following paragraph, or some of the students' paragraphs, on an overhead projector as you discuss the answers with the class.

Answers

1 Lee immigrated to Hawaii from Taiwan in 1956.
2 He learned English a long time ago.
3 He took classes at a community college for four years. / He took classes for four years at a community college.
4 Two years later, he started at the University of Hawaii.
5 In 1982, Lee graduated from the University of Hawaii.
6 From 1982 to 1992, he worked at a bank in Honolulu.
7 Lee moved to Philadelphia 10 years ago.
8 Four years later, Lee started a business.
9 For many years, Lee earned a lot of money.
10 Last year, Lee retired after many years of hard work. / Last year, after many years of hard work, Lee retired.

Lee immigrated to Hawaii from Taiwan in 1956. He learned English a long time ago. He took classes at a community college for four years. / He took classes for four years at a community college. Two years later, he started at the University of Hawaii. In 1982, Lee graduated from the University of Hawaii. From 1982 to 1992, he worked at a bank in Honolulu. Lee moved to Philadelphia 10 years ago. Four years later, Lee started a business. For many years, Lee earned a lot of money. Last year, Lee retired after many years of hard work. / Last year, after many years of hard work, Lee retired.

Practice 3 *page 119*

You may want to go over the time line with students before having them begin the exercise. When they are finished, have them compare their answers with a partner.

Answers

1 in 1988	3 three years later	5 for four years
2 in 1990	4 in 2006	6 a year later

B Learn more about the simple past pages 119–120

Write *go, do, have, make,* and *get* on the board. Ask students to make simple past sentences with those verbs. Point out that they are *irregular,* writing that term on the board. Explain that there are many irregular verbs in English as well as irregular verb patterns, but that it is best to try to memorize them little by little. Direct students' attention to the information box *Simple Past – Irregular Verbs* and have them follow along as you read the information. Pause to answer questions or clarify particular points. Elicit additional sentences for each verb.

Practice 4 page 120

Ask students if they know who Lorena Ochoa is, eliciting that she is a golfer. Bring in a picture from the Internet to show students who she is before having them begin the exercise. When they are finished, have them compare their answers with a partner. You may want to have students circle the irregular verbs in the paragraph.

Answers

1 was born	3 started	5 attended	7 lost	9 had	11 entered
2 grew up	4 won	6 played	8 became	10 won	12 started

Practice 5 page 120

Review with students the way to form the negative in the simple present by putting a simple present sentence on the board, such as *I go to Sanford City College now.* Have students change the sentence to the negative. Then ask them to put the affirmative sentence into the past, and elicit that *don't* or *do not* becomes *didn't* or *did not.* Call students' attention to the information box *Simple Past – Negative* and have them follow along as you read the information.

Look at the questions in *Practice 5* with students. Explain that there are many ways that they can answer these questions. Go over the first one and elicit a variety of answers before having students complete the exercise on their own. You may want to have volunteers put their sentences on the board while other students compare their answers in pairs.

Possible answers

1 I didn't go to the gym this morning.
2 I didn't speak English five years ago.
3 I didn't go to the movies last weekend.
4 I didn't move last year.
5 I didn't play sports in my childhood.

C Learn about paragraphs pages 121–122

Explain to students that they will be learning about paragraph structure and format from this chapter onward. Tell students that the structure of writing is different in all languages, but in English, all paragraphs have only one main idea. Direct students' attention to the information box *One Paragraph = One Idea* and read the information while students follow along. Have students read the paragraph on Duke Kahanamoku. After they finish, ask students what else might be interesting to read about in different paragraphs about this person, eliciting such topics as his education, his family life, his home, and so on. Point out that there are many other interesting topics, but that this paragraph is only talking about one topic, his Olympic swimming experiences.

Practice 6 *page 121*

Have students first read all of the sentences before rereading to find the sentences that don't belong. You may want to do the first one as a class before having students complete the second one on their own.

Answers

List A: Indonesian is a difficult language to learn. Punahou is very expensive and very large.

List B: We shared a bedroom. I was born in 1987. He is very smart.

Practice 7 *page 122*

Make sure students understand that there is only one answer for each item because each paragraph can only have one main idea. After going over the answers to *Practice 7*, you may want to go back to the answers to *Practice 6* and have students think of other sentences or pieces of information that could go in separate paragraphs about each one.

Answers

List A: c Obama's childhood

List B: b Ji-Sek, a great violinist

D Write the first draft *page 122*

For complete instructions, see page vi. Note that from this chapter onward, students will have a completed *Your turn* to help them with their first draft.

III REVISING YOUR WRITING

A Expand your vocabulary *page 123*

Put sentences on the board with some adverbs of time, such as *I woke up late, so I got up quickly.* Elicit from students that *quickly* is an adverb of time and that it modifies the verb *got up*. See if students know of any other adverbs of time before going over the material in the information box *More Adverbs* and eliciting additional examples for each adverb to check their comprehension. Point out the use of the comma.

Practice 8 page 123

You may want to do this exercise together as a class to check students' comprehension of the different adverbs.

Answers

1	gradually	4	quickly	7	quickly
2	Finally,	5	eventually		
3	Finally,	6	immediately		

B Connect your ideas page 124

Go over the information box *Using* Then, Next, *and* After That, having students read along with you and eliciting further example sentences. Make sure students notice the placement of the comma after *next* and *after that*. Write some sample sentences on the board without the comma and have students tell you where it goes.

Practice 9 page 124

Have students look at the picture of Lang Lang and elicit that he is a famous pianist before having them do the exercise. After completing the exercise, have students compare answers in pairs. Check for comma use with *next* and *after that*. Answers will vary; students do not need to use ordering words in every sentence. You may want to project the paragraph on an overhead projector and go over the answers with the class.

Possible answers

---

¹Lang Lang is a famous Chinese pianist. ²He began piano lessons at the age of three. ³ ~~H~~*Then h*e won the Shenyang Piano Competition at the age of five. ⁴*After that,* Lang Lang entered Beijing's Central Music Conservatory. ⁵He won an important music award at the age of 11. ⁶ ~~H~~*Next, h*e studied at the Curtis Institute in Philadelphia. ⁷Lang Lang played with the Los Angeles Symphony at 17. ⁸ ~~H~~*Then h*e performed at London's Royal Albert Hall in 2003.

C Give and get feedback page 125

Have students get into pairs and exchange their books and their first drafts. See page vii for more complete instructions.

D Write the second draft *page 125*

Have students use the feedback they just received to write a second draft. Remind them to refer to the charts that their partners filled in. See page vii for more complete instructions.

IV EDITING YOUR WRITING

A Focus on mechanics *page 126*

Go over the information box *Paragraph Format*. You may want to project this paragraph on an overhead projector to point out all the paragraph features to the students. Pay particular attention to sentences starting on the same line. Have students look back at all the other paragraphs in the book to find the features outlined here.

Practice 10 *page 126*

You may want to project this practice and a corrected paragraph on an overhead projector.

Answers

| 1 | 6 and 7, 9 and 10, 11 and 12 | 3 | 1 |
| 2 | 4, 5, 6, 11 | | |

B Check for common mistakes *page 127*

Mistakes with the simple past are common for many students. It takes a lot of practice on the students' part before mastering this. Go over the different categories of errors in the information box *Mistakes with the Simple Past*. If necessary, write additional sentences on the board with simple past errors and discuss them with the class before proceeding to *Practice 11*.

Practice 11 *page 127*

After students complete the exercise and compare their corrections with a partner, you many want to write the incorrect paragraph on the board for students to come up and correct, or project the paragraph on an overhead projector and make the corrections with the class.

Answers

> [1]My wife was born in 1980. [2]Her parents ~~die~~ _died_ two years later. [3]She ~~goed~~ _went_ to live with her grandparents. [4]She graduated high school in 1998, and then she ~~start~~ _started_ college. [5]She didn't ~~finished~~ _finish_ college. [6]After two years, she needed money, so she ~~stop~~ _stopped_. [7]She ~~get~~ _got_ a job in an office. [8]I also worked in that office. [9]We married two years later and ~~buy~~ _bought_ a big house.

C Edit your writing _page 127_

Have students look for and check each item on the checklist. Have them make their corrections directly on their draft.

D Write the final draft _page 128_

Have students incorporate all their mechanics edits into a final, polished draft. Remind students that they can make additional changes, if they wish.

V FOLLOWING UP

A Share your writing _page 128_

Go over the instructions with students. You may want to model the task by holding a student's time line and walking around the room asking key questions until you find the student whose time line you have. Then model comparing the time line with the paragraph.

B Check your progress _page 128_

Have students complete the _Progress Check_ and turn it in or show it to you.

Chapter 9 Going Places

In this chapter, students will write a paragraph about a trip that they have taken. They prepare for their first draft by working with topic-related vocabulary items and by learning about the simple past of *be* and time clauses with *before, after,* and *when*. They also learn how to develop ideas in a paragraph with general and specific sentences. After that, students expand their vocabulary by learning phrases for talking about the weather, and learn to connect ideas using *however*. They also study comma use when time words, expressions, and clauses begin a sentence. With your students, read the chapter introduction on page 129 and give students time to think about their answers to the questions.

I GETTING STARTED

A Useful vocabulary *page 130*

Elicit from students the part of speech that identifies all the words in the *Vocabulary Pool* (they're all adjectives). Review some of the common adjective endings (*-ing, -ful, -ive,* and so on).

Possible answers

Good Things: busy, cheap, cheerful, colorful, enjoyable, exciting, fascinating, fun, historic, lovely, peaceful, pleasant, popular, quiet, relaxing, safe

Bad Things: boring, crowded, dangerous, depressing, expensive, filthy, horrible, noisy, stressful, terrible, tiring, touristy, ugly, uncomfortable

B Vocabulary in context *page 131*

You may want to suggest that students underline words and phrases in the descriptions that help them complete the Good Things and Bad Things charts. Call on volunteers to share their answers with the class.

Answers

> **Top row:** 1, 2, 1
> **Bottom row:** 2, 1, 2
>
> **Paragraph 1**
> **Good Things:** The clothes were cheap, the museums were fascinating, the food was delicious, the hotel had a great pool
> **Bad Things:** The food was spicy, the weather wasn't very nice
>
> **Paragraph 2**
> **Good Things:** The hotel was cheap, the buildings were beautiful, the music was great
> **Bad Things:** It was crowded, things were expensive, the music was loud, we had headaches, breakfast wasn't very good

C Get ideas *page 132*

Allow plenty of time for students to discuss their charts. Circulate and offer help, if necessary.

D Freewrite *page 132*

Explain that students are going to use all the ideas they've been talking about, and any new words they remember, to freewrite about trips they have taken in the past. They are not limited to describing one trip. Encourage them to write down ideas about any trip or trips they want. For more complete freewriting instructions, see page v.

II PREPARING YOUR WRITING

A Learn about the simple past of *be* *page 133*

Write a topic-related sentence on the board with the simple present form of *be* and one with the verb missing, for example: *The hotel is comfortable. The hotel _____ comfortable.*

Then tell students a "story" about a great trip you took last year by saying something such as: *Last year, I went on a trip. Everything was great. For example, the hotel . . . .* Point to the third sentence. See if students can complete the sentence, supplying the correct past form of *be*.

Go over the information box *Using the Simple Past of* Be. To check comprehension, write several topic-related sentences on the board with different subjects and have students give you the correct past form of *be*.

Practice 1 *page 133*

Have students complete the exercise individually and then compare their answers with a partner.

Answers

1 weren't / were not
2 were, was

3 were, was
4 was, wasn't / was not

5 wasn't / was not, was
6 was, was

Practice 2 *page 133*

Answers

1 went
2 was
3 was
4 went
5 were
6 was

7 was
8 was
9 went
10 weren't / were not
11 was
12 watched

13 didn't go / did not go
14 wasn't / was not
15 was
16 was

B Learn about clauses *pages 134–135*

Write some sentences on the board that describe related events, such as: *I bought my ticket. I packed my suitcase. I went to the airport.*

Ask questions, such as: *What did I do first? What did I do second?* and so on. Then ask students how they might combine two events in one sentence, eliciting either *Before I packed my suitcase, I bought my ticket* or *I packed my suitcase after I bought my ticket*, and so on.

Direct students' attention to the information box *Using* Before, When, *and* After *in Clauses* and have them follow along as you read the information. To check their comprehension, put some sentences with time clauses on the board and ask students to identify the first and second events in each sentence.

Practice 3 *pages 134–135*

Suggest that students underline all the time words and expressions in the paragraph. Suggest that students write at least half of their answers with the time clause at the beginning of the sentence in order to reinforce comma use.

Answers

1 The Browns read a guidebook before they went to Puerto Rico. / Before they went to Puerto Rico, the Browns read a guidebook.
2 The weather was beautiful when they arrived. / When they arrived, the weather was beautiful.
3 The Browns went to the beach when they arrived. / When they arrived, the Browns went to the beach.
4 The Browns bought food, water, and gas before the hurricane came. / Before the hurricane came, the Browns bought food, water, and gas.
5 There were long lines at all the stores before the hurricane hit. / Before the hurricane hit, there were long lines at all the stores.
6 Everyone went indoors when the hurricane came. / When the hurricane came, everyone went indoors.

7 The Browns stayed indoors when the hurricane came. / When the hurricane came, the Browns stayed indoors.
8 Everything was calm after the hurricane ended. / After the hurricane ended, everything was calm.

Practice 4 *page 135*

Possible answers

Before she went to Rome, she applied for a passport / her friend gave her a book about Italy / her passport arrived.

When they were in Rome, they went to the National Museum / they went shopping / they ate a lot of delicious food / they met some students at the university / they took a lot of pictures.

After they arrived home, they were very tired / they got e-mails from Paolo and Mauro.

C Learn about paragraphs *pages 136–137*

Write a general statement on the board, such as *The weather is nice today*.

Explain that this is a general statement and see if students can give you a more specific statement about the weather, for example: *The sun is shining*, *It's warm*, *The sky is blue*, and so on. Elicit as many specific statements on the general topic as you can to illustrate that a general idea can be expanded with several related, specific ideas.

Direct students' attention to the information box *General and Specific Sentences* and have them follow along as you read. Make sure students understand the meaning of *general* and *specific*. Elicit additional examples for the General and Specific sentence lists at the bottom of the page.

Practice 5 *page 136*

You might want to have students do this exercise in pairs.

Answers

1 There were lots of beautiful clothing stores. There were many shoe stores, too.
2 The beds were uncomfortable. The rooms were small and dark.
3 The food was bad. The waiters were extremely rude.
4 They were cheap and on time. The seats were comfortable.
5 The sand was very clean. The water was warm and relaxing.

D Write the first draft *page 137*

For complete instructions, see page vi.

▌▌▌ REVISING YOUR WRITING

A Expand your vocabulary *pages 138–139*

Ask students to think of as many weather words as they can to describe the current weather conditions. Write them on the board. Then elicit some opposite or contrasting words for the current weather conditions.

Go over the information box *Weather Words* as students follow along. Have them repeat the example sentences.

Practice 6 *page 138*

Possible answers

1 d	2 f	3 b	4 c	5 e	6 a

Practice 7 *page 139*

You may want to have students underline words and phrases that describe the weather as they read.

Answers

1 d	2 c	3 e	4 b	5 a

B Connect your ideas *pages 139–140*

Write two sentences on the board that express contrasting ideas about a trip, such as: *The hotel was comfortable. It was expensive.*

Ask students if they can explain the relationship between the two sentences (they present contrasting ideas) and if they can think of a way to show the relationship not by combining them, but by adding one word to the beginning of the second sentence. Explain that in some cases, *but* is OK, but in formal, academic writing, we don't start a new sentence with *but*. Elicit or provide the new set of sentences: *The hotel was comfortable. However, it was expensive.*

Go over the information box *Using* However, For Example, *and* Because, having students repeat the examples and eliciting further example sentences. Make sure students notice the placement of the comma in sentences with *however*. Reinforce *however* and review *for example* and *because* by providing additional sets of sentences for students to revise using these connectors.

Practice 8 *page 140*

After completing the practice, have volunteers write the sentences on the board. Check for correct comma use.

Answers

1 However,	3 For example,	5 However,
2 because	4 For example,	6 because

C Give and get feedback *pages 140–141*

Have students get into pairs and exchange their books and their first drafts. See page vii for more complete instructions.

D Write the second draft *page 141*

Have students use the feedback they just received to write a second draft. Remind them to refer to the charts that their partners filled in. See page vii for more complete instructions.

IV EDITING YOUR WRITING

A Focus on mechanics *pages 141–142*

Write two or three trip-related sentences on the board with time expressions, leaving out the commas. Ask students if they see anything wrong with them.

Go over the information box *Using Commas with Time Words, Expressions, and Clauses*. To check students' understanding, write additional examples of sentences with time expressions at the ends of the sentences. Have students come to the board and rewrite them with the time expression at the beginning of the sentence.

Practice 9 *page 142*

Answers

> [1]Last July, we went to San Francisco for our vacation. [2]Before we left, we packed our suitcases. [3]We packed lots of shorts, T-shirts, and sandals. [4]After that, we went to the airport. [5]When we got to the airport, we checked our bags and went to the gate. [6]The flight was late. [7]We waited at the gate for four hours! [8]Finally, our plane took off. [9]We arrived in San Francisco very late at night. [10]After we arrived, we went to get our suitcases, but they weren't there. [11]They were lost! [12]We filled out a lot of forms at the airport. [13]It was midnight! [14]Finally, we left the airport. [15]We took the subway, but we got lost. [16]About two hours later, we found our hotel. [17]When we woke up the next day, our suitcases were at the hotel. [18]We were happy. [19]However, the weather was terrible! [20]It was cold and rainy every day, so we bought some warm clothes!

B Check for common mistakes *pages 142–143*

Go over the information box *Forming the Simple Past*. Write additional sentences on the board with simple past errors and discuss them with the class.

Practice 10 *page 143*

Write the incorrect paragraph on the board for students to come up and correct, or project the paragraph on an overhead projector and make the corrections with the class.

Answers

> ¹Two years ago, we ~~were climb~~ *climbed* Mt. Fuji in Japan. ²Before we ~~were go,~~ *went* we read a lot of books. ³We packed all the right clothes. ⁴We ~~were take~~ *took* bottles of water and lots of snacks. ⁵They were really heavy! ⁶When we ~~were get~~ *got* to the mountain, we saw a lot of snack bars. ⁷We ~~weren't~~ *didn't* need all our food!

C Edit your writing *page 143*

Have students look for and check each item on the checklist. Have them make their corrections directly on their draft.

D Write the final draft *page 143*

Have students incorporate all their mechanics edits into a final, polished draft. Remind students that they can make additional changes, if they wish.

V FOLLOWING UP

A Share your writing *page 144*

Make sure that students give reasons for their rankings. You might want to have each group report on the highest-rated trip in their group, and then rank the top trips for the entire class.

B Check your progress *page 144*

Have students complete the *Progress Check* and turn it in or show it to you.

In the Future

In this chapter, students produce a paragraph about their plans for the future. The first part of this chapter is different from all the rest as they prepare for their first drafts by completing a *Vocabulary Pool* box with topic-related vocabulary items they have studied in previous chapters, or words they already know that they think will be useful. This will serve as a review of much of the vocabulary in the relevant chapters. They also prepare for their first drafts by learning about forming sentences with the simple future using *going to* and also by using the verbs *plan, expect, intend, hope,* and *want* + *to* + verb. After that, students learn about topic sentences and expand their vocabulary by learning future time expressions. They also learn to connect their ideas using ordering words to show the order of events. Finally, students learn about writing titles for their paragraphs and to correct common errors with forming the future with verb + *to*. With your students, read the chapter introduction on page 145 and give students time to think about their answers to the questions.

I GETTING STARTED

A Useful vocabulary page 146

Ask students what is different about this page, pointing out that the *Vocabulary Pool* is almost empty. Explain that they are going to find words in the book that they think will be useful for their paragraphs. Explain that in this way, they will be reviewing much of the vocabulary in the book. Give students extra time to compare answers as it is likely they will have chosen different vocabulary items and that they have provided different words of their own.

B Vocabulary in context page 147

Check students' comprehension of *short-* and *long-term*, giving real-world examples of actual goals in the students' lives or in your life.

Answers

| 1 c, short-term | 2 a, long-term | 3 d, long-term |

C Get ideas *page 148*

You may want to elicit from the students different types of short- and long-term goals and plans.

D Freewrite *page 148*

Explain that students are going to use all the ideas they've been talking about, and any new words they remember, to freewrite about their future plans. For more complete freewriting instructions, see page v.

II PREPARING YOUR WRITING

A Learn about the simple future with *going to* *pages 149–150*

Write a topic-related sentence on the board about a plan in the future with a blank in front of the verb, such as *I _____ study Spanish next semester.* Elicit from students that this is a plan for something in the future, and ask them what should go in the blank, eliciting *am going to*. If students say *will*, tell them that *will* is another way to talk about the future, but that it is not used for future plans. Have students tell you some of their plans while you write them on the board with *be going to*.

Call students' attention to the information box *Using Going To* and have them follow along as you read the information. Pause to answer questions or clarify particular points. Pay particular attention to the fact that the negative is formed with the *be* verb. Have students make sentences of their own in the affirmative and in the negative.

Practice 1 *page 149*

Check that students understand that the only verb they need to change is *be*. They may use the full or contracted form.

Possible answers

1 are going to have	4 isn't going to work	7 are going to study
2 are going to move	5 am going to save	8 are not going to graduate
3 is going to get	6 am not going to take	

Practice 2 *page 150*

Go over the verb choices with students before they complete the exercise. They may use either the full or the contracted form of *be*.

Possible answers

1 am going to finish	4 am going to look	7 are going to move
2 am going to live	5 isn't going to be	
3 am going to apply	6 am not going to work	

B Learn about *plan, expect, intend, hope, want* + *to* + verb   *pages 150–151*

Explain that there are other ways to express future plans in English. Write the following sentence on the board: *I plan to go to Hawaii next summer.* Elicit that this is a present simple sentence but that it is another way to express a plan in the future even though it is written in the present simple tense. Write the words *plan, expect, intend, hope,* and *want* + *to* + verb on the board. Tell students that they can use these words instead of *be* + *going* + *to* + verb. Direct students' attention to the information box *Using* Plan, Expect, Intend, Hope, Want + To + Verb and have them follow along as you read the information. Pause to answer questions or clarify particular points about the differences in meaning. Elicit additional sentences for each verb. If needed, you could put a continuum line on the board with *very sure* on the right side and *not very sure* on the left and have students place the verbs on the continuum.

Practice 3 *page 151*

Check that students understand what certificate courses are and have them say what they think a Green Gardener certificate might be, eliciting that it is a certificate for someone who gardens ecologically and in an environmentally aware way. Draw students' attention to the capitalization of *Green Gardener* so they notice that it is a proper name of a certificate. Have students read the sentences first before rereading them to put them in order and completing the exercise.

Possible answers

1 I intend to get a certificate in Green Gardening.
2 I want to have my own business.
3 I hope to open a Green Gardening business.
4 I intend to work for a gardening business.
5 I plan / expect to finish my English studies.
6 I intend to take landscaping classes at a local college.

Practice 4 *page 151*

Go over the instructions with students. You may want to have students do this exercise in class so that you can circulate to offer help, as needed. You may want to project students' finished paragraphs and the sample one below on an overhead projector to compare possible answers.

Possible answer

My Own Business

In five years, I want to have my own business. First, I plan / expect to finish my English studies. After that, I intend to take landscaping classes at a local college. At the end of the course, I intend to get a certificate in Green Gardening. After I get my certificate, I intend to work for a gardening business in my hometown. Finally, when I have enough experience and enough money, I hope to open a Green Gardening business.

C Learn about paragraphs *page 152*

Review with students the fact that every paragraph has only one main idea. Explain that this idea is usually stated in a sentence, which is called a *topic sentence*. Illustrate the difference between a topic and a topic sentence for students by looking back at the paragraph they wrote for *Practice 4*. Tell them that the topic is *having a business* but that the topic sentence gives more specific information about that topic. Direct students' attention to the information box *Topic Sentences* and read the information while the students follow along. To practice, you may want to have the students look at paragraphs in previous chapters to state the topic and to read the topic sentences.

Practice 5 *page 152*

After going over the answers, ask students to say why the other options were not good topic sentences for this paragraph. You may want to have students say what the information would be in a paragraph with those topic sentences.

Answers

| 2, 5

D Write the first draft *page 153*

For complete instructions, see page vi.

III REVISING YOUR WRITING

A Expand your vocabulary *pages 153–154*

Have students look back at previous paragraphs in this chapter and find future time phrases. Call students' attention to the information box *Future Time Expressions* and read through the phrases in the definite and indefinite lists. Go over the meaning of each phrase in the definite and indefinite lists, eliciting additional examples for each time expression to check students' comprehension. Point out the use of the comma.

Practice 6 *page 153*

Have student volunteers write their sentences on the board while other students compare theirs in pairs.

Possible answers

| In two years, Lucia expects to get a business degree at the university.
| In four years, she plans to move to New York City.
| She intends to apply for a job at a small business in New York in five years.
| In the future, she hopes to get promoted at my job.
| Later on, she wants to have a house with a big yard and three children.
| She hopes to travel around Asia one day.

B Connect your ideas *pages 154–155*

Go over the information box *Ordering Words*, having students follow along
as you read the information. Make sure students notice the placement of the
comma. Write some sample sentences on the board without the comma and
have students tell you where it goes. Also, illustrate how these words were used
in Chapter 8 in a similar way.

Practice 7 *page 154*

Point out to students that the ordering words are only used three and four times
in the two paragraphs.

Possible answers

Paragraph 1:	1 First	2 Then	3 Finally	
Paragraph 2:	1 First	2 Next	3 Then	4 Finally

C Give and get feedback *page 155*

Have students get into pairs and exchange their books and their first drafts. See
page vii for more complete instructions.

D Write the second draft *page 155*

Have students use the feedback they just received to write a second draft. Remind
them to refer to the charts that their partners filled in. See page vii for more
complete instructions.

IV EDITING YOUR WRITING

A Focus on mechanics *pages 156–157*

Go over the information box *Writing Titles*. Point out that titles are more similar
to topics than they are to topic sentences. You may want to have students look
back to paragraphs in previous chapters and give them titles.

Practice 8 *page 156*

Ask students which titles sound the most interesting to them.

Answers

1 Hopes and Dreams for a Nurse
2 My Plan for My Family
3 Saving Money for a House
4 Getting a Job Teaching Young Children
5 A Trip to Costa Rica Next Summer

Practice **9** *pages 156–157*

Have students give reasons for their choice of title.

Answers

> **Topic sentence:** I hope to work in many countries for the next 10 years.
> **Title:** (c) Working Overseas as an Engineer

Practice **10** *page 157*

Have students do the exercise in class. Then have students tell the class their titles and give reasons for their choices. You might want to put the titles on the board and have students vote on the best one.

Possible answers

> **Paragraph 1:** Moving to Seattle
> **Paragraph 2:** Becoming a Private Chef

B Check for common mistakes *pages 157–158*

Mistakes with the future are common for many students as there are quite a few things to remember. Go over the different categories of mistakes in the information box *Forming the Future with Verb + To*. If necessary, write additional sentences on the board with similar errors and discuss them with the class before proceeding to *Practice 11*.

Practice **11** *page 158*

Suggest that students refer back to the information box as they look for the errors. After students complete the exercise and compare their corrections with a partner, you may want to write the incorrect paragraph on the board for students to come up and correct, or project the paragraph on an overhead projector and make the corrections with the class.

Answers

Having a Family

¹In two years, my boyfriend and I ~~am~~ *are* going to get married. ²We want to finish school first. ³I expect *to* ˄finish school in two years, but my boyfriend plans to ~~finishes~~ *finish* next year. ⁴Then we intend ˄*to* look for jobs. ⁵We hope to find jobs in Tokyo. ⁶We ˄*are* going to look for jobs in the same area. ⁷After that, we are going ˄*to* look for an apartment. ⁸We both want ˄*to* live close to our work. ⁹Finally, we are ~~go~~ *going* to get married. ¹⁰We hope to have our wedding in Hawaii. ¹¹We want to ~~having~~ *have* a beautiful wedding!

C Edit your writing *page 158*

Have students look for and check each item on the checklist. Have them make their corrections directly on their draft.

D Write the final draft *page 159*

Have students incorporate all their mechanics edits into a final, polished draft. Remind students that they can make additional changes, if they wish.

V FOLLOWING UP

A Share your writing *page 159*

Go over the instructions with students in advance so they can bring their sentence strips to class. You may want to take the students to a computer lab if your school has one.

Model the task by putting sentence strips of your own on the board. Have students practice finding the topic sentence and ordering the remaining sentences.

B Check your progress *page 160*

Have students complete the *Progress Check* and turn it in or show it to you.